The Scholarship on Spanish Mystical Literature

Brill Research Perspectives in Religion and the Arts

Editor-in-Chief

Aaron Rosen (*Wesley Theological Seminary, Washington, DC*)

Associate Editors

Barbara Baert (*University of Leuve*)
Yohana A. Junker (*Pacific School of Religion, Berkeley*)
S. Brent Plate (*Hamilton College, New York*)
Zhange Ni (*Virginia Tech*)

Founding Editor

Diane Apostolos-Cappadona (*Georgetown University, Washington, DC*)

Volumes published in this Brill Research Perspective title are listed at *brill.com/rpra*

The Scholarship on Spanish Mystical Literature

Through an Orientalist Lens

By

Gloria Maité Hernández

BRILL

LEIDEN | BOSTON

This paperback book edition is simultaneously published as issue 4.4 (2020) of *Brill Research Perspectives in Religion and the Arts*, DOI: 10.1163/24688878-12340014.

Library Congress Control Number: 2021922230

Typeface for the Latin, Greek, and Cyrillic scripts: "Brill". See and download: brill.com/brill-typeface.

ISBN 978-90-04-50957-3 (paperback)
ISBN 978-90-04-50956-6 (e-book)

Copyright 2021 by Gloria Maité Hernández. Published by Koninklijke Brill NV, Leiden, The Netherlands.
Koninklijke Brill NV incorporates the imprints Brill, Brill Nijhoff, Brill Hotei, Brill Schöningh, Brill Fink, Brill mentis, Vandenhoeck & Ruprecht, Böhlau Verlag and V&R Unipress.
Koninklijke Brill NV reserves the right to protect this publication against unauthorized use. Requests for re-use and/or translations must be addressed to Koninklijke Brill NV via brill.com or copyright.com.

This book is printed on acid-free paper and produced in a sustainable manner.

Contents

The Scholarship on Spanish Mystical Literature
Through an Orientalist Lens 1
    Gloria Maité Hernández
  Abstract 1
  Keywords 1
  Introduction 2
1 Mysticism and Orientalism 8
  1.1 *Mysticism: A Concept in the Making* 8
      1.1.1 *Philosophia Perennia*: William James 11
      1.1.2 Evelyn Underhill: The Prominence of Christian Mysticism 13
      1.1.3 From Mystical Experience to Mystical Language 15
      1.1.4 Michel De Certeau: Mystical Language and the Spanish Exception 18
  1.2 *Spanish Orientalism* 20
2 The Scholarship on Spanish Mystical Literature Pre-1942 23
  2.1 *Marcelino Menéndez Pelayo and the Terror of the Orient* 23
  2.2 *Miguel Asín Palacios: Mysticism, Orientalism, and Comparison* 26
      2.2.1 A Historical Approach 27
      2.2.2 Comparison by Analogy 29
      2.2.3 The New Disciplines of Comparative Philology and Comparative Religion 30
      2.2.4 Asín Palacio's Internal and External Orientalisms 33
  2.3 *The External Orientalism of Edgar Allison Peers* 34
      2.3.1 Edgar Allison Peers vs. Otis Green 37
3 The Scholarship on Spanish Mystical Literature: 1942 and the Next Two Decades 42
  3.1 *Dámaso Alonso and the "Italian Thesis"* 42
      3.1.1 The Alonso–Peers Debate 43
  3.2 *Helmut Hatzfeld and the "National Tendencies of Mystical Language"* 45
  3.3 *Ángel Cilveti and the "Patrimony of Spanish Culture"* 48

4 The Scholarship on Spanish Mystical Literature: The Turn
of the Century   51
  4.1   *Luce López-Baralt: From "Where?" to "What?"*   51
  4.2   *José Ángel Valente: Beyond Transmission and Convergences*   54
    4.2.1 José Ángel Valente on the Language of the Mystics   59
  4.3   *Eulogio Pacho: Relations and Dependencies*   62
  Conclusions: The Scholarship on Spanish Mystical Literature:
  Its Present and Future   64
  Works Cited   69
  General Bibliography   72

The Scholarship on Spanish Mystical Literature
Through an Orientalist Lens

Gloria Maité Hernández
West Chester University, West Chester, Pennsylvania, USA
gloriamaite@gmail.com

Abstract

An engaging critical review is offered of scholarly works on Spanish mystical literature during the twentieth and early twenty-first century in Europe and the Americas. Bringing together for the first time an ample variety of sources, and letting the scholars' own voices be heard, this study asks how their writings were influenced by their particular notions about mysticism and Spain's relationship with the Orient. A thematic survey like this one illustrates how ideas are created and re-created throughout time, resulting in the production of a more diverse scholarship. Readers will be enriched with a renewed sense of disciplinary awareness.

Keywords

Orientalism – Mysticism – Spanish mysticism – Spanish mystical literature – Saint John of the Cross/San Juan de la Cruz – Saint Teresa of Jesus/Santa Teresa de Jesús – Marcelino Menéndez Pelayo – Edgar Allison Peers – Otis Green – Miguel Asín Palacios – Luce López-Baralt – José Ángel Valente – Dámaso Alonso – Eulogio Pacho – Ángel Cilveti

∙∙∙

To Luce López-Baralt, who once told me that being Latin Americans allows us to write as we do about Spanish mystical literature

∙∙∙

Hombre occidental, tu miedo al oriente, ¿es miedo a morir o a despertar?

∴

Western man, your fear of the Orient, is it a fear of sleeping or waking up?*,1

ANTONIO MACHADO

∴

Introduction

In 1924, a British scholar publishes the first book on Spanish mystical literature in English in order to reveal to the world the richness of the Spanish mystical tradition, which has not yet been fully realized even by the Spaniards themselves. He starts this book by evoking the image of a foreign traveler in Spain who immediately discovers that mysticism is inherent to the Spanish people. In 1931, a Spanish scholar and Catholic priest publishes *Islam Cristianizado* (*Christianized Islam*), where he argues that the writings of the two best-known Spanish mystical writers, Saint John of the Cross and Saint Teresa of Jesus, display Sufi influences – not because the Spanish saints were directly exposed to Sufi writings, but because Sufis were influenced by early Christians, and therefore were themselves Christians without knowing it. In 1938, an American scholar sets out to contest the Englishman's viewpoints. He affirms that the sixteenth-century Spanish mystical writers were neither influenced by non-Spanish sources nor were a product of the "innate mysticism" of Spaniards but "a literary generation" created by "the leadership of genius."[2] The British scholar responds to the American in 1942, insisting that the Spanish are indeed "mystically-minded people" and that it is enough to visit a Spanish church for one hour in the early morning "to grasp one of the first principles of the mystical life."[3] In 1942 and in 1946, a young Spanish scholar rebuts the Spaniard, the Briton, and the American, promoting the so-called "Italian

---

* I thank the anonymous reviewer for her or his generous and supportive comments.
1 Unless otherwise noted, all translations from Spanish into English that appear in this volume are by the author.
2 Otis Green, "The Historical Problem of Castilian Mysticism," 103.
3 Edgar Allison Peers, "Notes on the Historical Problem of Castilian Mysticism," 21.

thesis," which attributes the greatness of Spanish mystical poetry to Italian and Romanized sources.

This scholarly back-and-forth, which extended longer than the quarter century summarized above, demonstrates that the ideas of twentieth-century scholars about Spanish mystical literature were built upon two notions: more apparently, their thoughts about mysticism itself; and more covertly, their view of the place that Spain occupied in the geo-political European map, particularly in relation to the part of the world they assumed to be "the Orient." Their most burning questions of debate was an orientalist question: who influenced Spanish mystical writers, and how did such influences affect the ideal of the "true" mystical and Christian character of the Spanish culture?

These two non-static notions of mysticism and orientalism will frame the present critical review. Today, scholars of mystical literature agree on the modern definition of mysticism as the element within Christianity and within other religious traditions "that concerns the preparation for, the attainment of, and the effect of what is described as an immediately conscious 'presence' of God."[4] But this description would sound strange to sixteenth-century Spanish mystical writers, and also to early and mid-twentieth-century scholars who wrote about Spanish mystical literature. Authors like Saint John of the Cross and Saint Teresa of Jesus used not the term "mysticism" but *teología mística*, a translation of the Greek phrase *theologia mystikē* deployed by the sixth-century Syrian Christian monk known as Dionysius the Areopagite to describe the secret or hidden (*mustikos*) knowledge of God (*theologia*). Conversely, twentieth-century scholars of Spanish mysticism referred to mysticism as a practice, an event specifically related to the union with God, or an experience that is mostly particular to the Christian tradition. They would also emphasize the importance of differentiating between mystical and religious writings as the former are characterized by claiming some kind of direct experience of the divine, which the latter do not.

The second key concept that frames this study, one possibly more familiar to the reader, is the modern notion of orientalism in the classic definition by Edward Said as "the stage on which the whole East is confined."[5] However, in the case of the Iberian Peninsula, and specifically in the case of Spain, the concept of orientalism is complicated by paradoxical orientalist practices, well described by César Domínguez as "internal" and "external" modes of orientalism.[6] Within Spain, we find a self-confined orientalism, where "oriental" is the term used by Spanish scholars to define their internal "others,"

---

4 Michael Kessler and Christian Sheppard, eds., *Mystics: Presence and Aporia*, viii.
5 Edward Said, *Orientalism*, 63.
6 César Domínguez, "The South European Other: A Comparative Reflection on Space in Literary History."

mainly Muslims and Jews. In the twentieth century, this practice of internal orientalism was dominated by nationalist discourses aimed at hiding the internal "oriental" from the eye of the European outsider. Outside Spain, we find that "oriental" is precisely the term used by the rest of Europe in reference to Spain during the nineteenth and early twentieth century. While the late twentieth-century notion of orientalism was not yet in play in the context of most of the scholars whose works I will examine here, their orientalist biases, in their peculiar internal and external modalities, will help us comprehend why they wrote as they did about Spanish mystical writers. At certain points in this volume, I have also deployed the term "geo-politics" to refer to scholars' ideas not just about the position of Spain in relation to the Orient but in relation to Europe and the rest of the world.

Focused on the concepts of mysticism and orientalism – with their dynamic definitions – this survey study will examine the scholarship on Spanish mystical literature produced inside and outside Spain during the twentieth and the first years of the twenty-first century. We will analyze how scholars' ideas about "the oriental" determined their methods for approaching Spanish mystical writings. Conversely, we will observe how, as the notions of mysticism and orientalism transformed, so their methodological approaches to Spanish mystical literature changed, and the scholarly questions moved, slowly but steadily, beyond the orientalist quest. In general, the goal of this study is two-fold. First, it is to bring into today's field of Spanish mystical literature an awareness of the geo-political biases that permeate the work of the scholars that we still read, cite, and teach. Secondly, without losing perspective of how much we can still learn from their work, it is to understand the foundations of these scholars' biases and commitments so that we may make more informed methodological decisions in order to revitalize the field of Spanish mystical literature.

It would be challenging to appreciate the orientalist dynamics of the scholarship on Spanish mystical literature without some knowledge of Spain's particular historical background. While this is not the place for a lengthy discussion of how a part of the Iberian Peninsula became today's Spain, I will focus here on two years: 1492, which marks the beginning of the Spanish Catholic Empire that defined itself by opposition to the oriental; and 1942, which marks the apogee of the Franco dictatorship and the 500th anniversary of the birth of Saint John of the Cross, an event that the Franco regime employed to reaffirm the exclusivist Catholic character of Spain. Readers familiar with Spain's history may bypass the next three paragraphs.

The Spanish Catholic monarchy was established in the last decade of the fifteenth century with the marriage of Isabel of Castile and Fernando of León. The Holy Office of the Inquisition had been brought to Spain by their royal predecessors in 1478. By the end of the fifteenth century, the Inquisition had become a powerful institution, exercising economic and political control alongside the crown. Together, the Catholic monarchs and the Inquisition embarked on a war against the Muslim kingdoms which remained from the glorious Umayyad Empire of Al-Andalus, founded in the southern portion of the Peninsula in the tenth century and which occupied the province known today as Andalusia. The last city under Muslim rule, Granada, was taken over by the Catholic monarchs in January of 1492. In March of the same year, the royal house published the "Edict of Expulsion of the Jews," offering the Jewish population the choice of conversion or exile. The official expulsion day of the Jews from Iberia would be the second of August, the exact day when Christopher Columbus sailed in search of "the Indies," supported by the favor and the wealth of the Catholic monarchs. Also in August of 1492, the *First Grammar of the Castilian Language* was published by Antonio de Nebrija. This document contributed to the official declaration of Spanish as the language of the Empire and was dedicated to Queen Isabel "because language was always the companion [*compañera*] of empire."[7] In October, Columbus arrived at the "New World," thus embarking on the colonial enterprise that made Spain the center of the most powerful kingdom of its time. The events briefly listed above established the foundation of the Spanish Empire which, from its very beginning, defined itself by opposition to the "oriental," specifically the Muslims and Jews who inhabited in the Peninsula, those who chose exile after being expelled or forced to convert, as well as those who lived in North Africa.

Four and a half centuries later, the National Catholic ideology promoted by the Francisco Franco regime was in many ways parallel to that advanced by the Spanish Monarchy for the establishment of the Empire. The dictatorship of Francisco Franco (1936–1975) had determined some of its most relevant features during the Spanish Civil War (1936–1939), characterized by the role of Franco as the *caudillo*. The political measures adopted during the years of the Civil War and the early post-war era were marked by the rhetoric of a triumphant fascism, which Francoists called National-Catholicism. Franco created the sole political party led by the FET (Falange Española Tradicionalista), the JONS (Juntas de Ofensiva Nacional Sindicalista), and the sector of the militant Catholic Church which supported the regime. The goal of the national Catholic leadership of the Franco dictatorship was to make Spain "great again." That meant purely Catholic and Castilian. To attain this, one of their means was to

---

7 Antonio de Nebrija, *The Prologue to Grammar of the Castilian Language* (1492). In "On Language and Empire: The Prologue to Grammar of the Castilian Language (1492)," 202.

erase every cultural trace that would identify Spain as "oriental," especially in regard to North African Muslims from the other side of the Strait of Gibraltar.[8]

The year 1942 was particularly triumphant for the sector of the Spanish Catholic Church which supported the Franco regime. Together, the Church and a group of intellectuals set out to grandly celebrate the five-hundredth anniversary of the birth of one of Spain's most controversial mystical writers, Saint John of the Cross. Besides the many religious commemorations, the anniversary celebrations included the publication of a number of academic articles and books dedicated to his life and work. In the words of the late twentieth-century writer José Ángel Valente, the historical circumstances of 1942 allowed for "the association of the religious or the sacred with limiting and threatening determinants of fear."[9] Such limits and fears, imposed by the Franco rule, mandated directly or indirectly the scholarly approaches to Spanish mystical writers. As a result, the massive amount of scholarship on Saint John of the Cross and on Spanish mystical literature in general produced in and around 1492 was, in Valente's words, "mutilated beforehand" by an official discourse seeking to reaffirm an image of Spain as exclusively Catholic and inserted within the European Romanized cultural tradition.[10] Again, the question leading the scholarship produced during in this period was not how or what these mystic authors wrote but where to find their sources of influence. For scholars within Spain, writing and publishing under the surveillance of the Franco regime and within the coordinates of the internal orientalism it promoted, the task was to locate sources that proved the exclusively European traces of the Spanish mystics.

The present extended survey article is organized according to a chronological structure within a conceptual framework. Chronologically, we will analyze the scholarship of Spanish mystical literature throughout three specific moments in time: the early years of the twentieth century previous to 1942; the mid-twentieth century, including the scholarship produced during 1942; and the late twentieth and early twenty-first century. Obviously, it has been impossible to include each publication about Spanish mystical literature. While some crucial contributions have had to be omitted, I have selected a group of scholars from each time period that reflects both the work produced inside and outside Spain and an encompassing perspective on the question of internal and external orientalism. Closely examining their work will allow us

---

8   The causes and consequences of this historical reinvention have been widely discussed by historians such as Américo Castro and scholars like Marcel Bataillon, as well as by writers like Juan Goytisolo.
9   José Ángel Valente, "Formas de lectura," 16.
10 José Ángel Valente, Hermenéutica, 20.

to observe how the dynamics of internal and external orientalism in regard to Spain determined the methods and critical approaches that scholars employed to write about Spanish mystical literature.

According to the structure describe above, this volume is divided into four parts: first, a general overview of the scholarly development of the two concepts that will guide the analysis, namely mysticism and orientalism, during the twentieth and early twenty-first centuries. In that first section, we will refer to those ideas which helped to shape the very notion of mysticism as understood by those who wrote – and write today – about Spanish mystical literature. The scholarship on Spanish mystical literature has moved both in parallel with and oblique to the development of the concept of mysticism in Western scholarship. Alongside the changing concept of mysticism, we will analyze the notion of orientalism. While the general Saidian concept of the oriental requires less of a thorough introduction, I will look into the peculiar orientalists' dynamics in relation to the Spanish territory, thoroughly described by César Domínguez. From Domínguez I will borrow the notions of internal and external orientalism as the framework for critically reviewing the scholarship on Spanish mystical literature to be developed in the rest of the study.

The second section will turn to the work of scholars on Spanish mystical literature. To give the reader a taste of the actual scholarly texts, I have cited relevant passages, most of them in my own English translations. First, we will discuss diverse examples of the scholarship on Spanish mysticism produced inside and outside Spain before 1942. This section starts not in the twentieth century but in 1881, with the speech offered by one of the most renowned Spanish scholars of all times, Marcelino Menéndez-Pelayo, at his induction into the Royal Academy of the Spanish Language. I find in Menéndez-Pelayo's speech the seeds of the strong correlation between the concepts of mysticism and the oriental in the critique of Spanish mystical literature. Next, I attend to the work of the Spanish scholar and father of Spanish Islamic Studies, Miguel Asín Palacios; the British scholar Edgar Allison Peers; and the American scholar Otis Green.

The third part will consider the scholarship produced around the 1942 celebrations for the five-hundredth anniversary of Saint John of the Cross's birth, and extending to the next three decades of Francoism. This section begins by examining the latest work of Spanish scholar Dámaso Alonso and his debates with the English Edgar Allison Peers. We will also analyze the work of the German scholar Helmut Hatzfeld and the Spaniard-American Ángel Cilveti, each featuring a distinct approach to the orientalist enterprise. Cilveti's work will serve as a bridge to the final part of the volume, focused on the work of scholars Luce López-Baralt, José Ángel Valente, and Eulogio Pacho. In these scholars, we encounter the call for a new attitude toward the question of the sources of the Spanish mystical writers and the movement toward a comparative approach to mystical texts that takes the field beyond the orientalist question that prevailed in the earlier scholarship. To conclude, I will bring together the chronological and conceptual notions surveyed throughout the volume; I will refer to some of the work produced nowadays within and outside Spain on Spanish mystical literature; and I will advance some of the scholarly implications produced by a study like this one.

This detailed examination of scholarship about Spanish mystical literature may provoke further inquiry in scholars whose work is not necessarily engaged with this specific topic. For someone interested in the history of thought, for example, this volume offers a case study on one topic viewed from diverse historical, philosophical, and religious perspectives. Moreover, a thematic survey like this one illustrates how ideas are created and re-created throughout time, resulting in the production of a more diverse scholarship. Embedded in twentieth-century scholars' arguments about Spanish mystical literature are not only their notions about Spain's geo-political position in the European map but also their thoughts about religion, history, writing; and about the very reason for doing scholarly work.

A student or a scholar of Spanish mystical literature, whether or not she or he wants to engage with the orientalist argument that frames this survey, can gather from it a variety of research data with ample reference to primary and secondary sources. For those with a more committed investment in the field of Spanish mystical literature or of Spanish literature in general, this essay opens a window through which we can examine ourselves. After reading this volume, I would expect my reader to feel enriched with a sense of disciplinary awareness. Knowing how and why the scholarship edifice on Spanish mystical literature has been built, we, as twenty-first-century scholars called to move the field forward, can ask what our tasks are. If there is something new to write about Spanish mystical works, what is it, and from what perspective should we approach it? How are we negotiating our own biases and commitments to our topic of study? What are our own agendas in a post-orientalist and post-colonial scholarship context? And how do we respond to the increasing need for a dialogue with other disciplines, methodologies, and religious traditions?

1   Mysticism and Orientalism

1.1   *Mysticism: A Concept in the Making*
In his *Tesoro de la lengua Española* – the first monolingual Spanish dictionary, published in 1611 – Sebastián de Covarrubias defines the word *místico* ("mystic") in relation to *misterio* ("mystery"), and *misterio* as "anything that is

hidden behind a veil, or facts, or words, or other signs."[11] One of the greatest sixteenth-century Spanish mystics, Saint John of the Cross – who died two decades before the publication of Covarrubias's dictionary – would probably have agreed to define mysticism as an experience that is hidden behind signs. However, neither Saint John of the Cross nor Saint Teresa of Jesus – the other great Spanish mystical writer – spoke of or wrote about "mysticism." Instead, they used the Dionysian term *teología mística*. Building on Neoplatonic sources and on Origen's commentary on the Biblical *Song of Songs*, Dionysius the Areopagite was the first one to offer a dialectical understanding primarily in terms of God as Eros. For Dionysius, God goes "out of himself in a complete ecstasy of self-giving because he alone has the ability to remain absolutely within himself."[12] The implied "differentiated union" contained within God's "self-giving" love can be grasped, according to Dionysius, by means of a cataphatic method (from the Greek *kataphaticos* ("affirmative speech") or by an apophatic method (from the Greek *apophatikos* – "denying speech"). Of these two, the apophatic method, which goes beyond reason, is what Dionysius called mystical theology.[13] As Covarrubias aptly puts it in his dictionary, Dionysius's choice of the term "mystical" – from the Greek *mustikos*, "hidden, secret" – is the root of what came to be known as mysticism, often discussed alongside the linguistic categories of apophatic and cataphatic: ineffable or put into words, respectively.

The modern North American scholar of mysticism Bernard McGinn finds it "utopian" to define mysticism. In lieu of a definition, he presents three notions that may guide the study of mystical texts: first, that mysticism is "a part or element of religion." Mystics are not found in isolation from any specific religious traditions but as a part of a tradition which they profess. Secondly, mysticism should be thought of as "a process and a way of life." Although mysticism "may be conceived of as a particular kind of encounter between God and the human, between Infinite Spirit and the finite human spirit," every part of the process that guides the person toward the encounter with God can also be considered as "mystical."[14] And finally, while most scholarship on mysticism – and on the mystical experience – focuses on the moment of union between the person and God as the culminating, experiential point of the mystical experience, McGinn argues that "union with God is not the most central category for understanding mysticism." Instead, he turns attention to the notion of "presence," particularly an awareness or "consciousness" of divine presence.

---

11   Sebastián de Covarrubias, *Tesoro de la lengua castellana o española*, 551.
12   Bernard McGinn, *The Foundations of Mysticism: Origins to the Fifth Century*, 167.
13   McGinn, 163.
14   McGinn, xvi.

He writes that "the mystical element in Christianity" is the "belief and practices that concerns the preparation for, the consciousness of, and the reaction to what can be described as the immediate or direct presence of God."[15] This presence, which:

> [D]efies conceptualization and verbalization ... can only be presented indirectly, partially, by a series of verbal strategies in which language is used not so much informationally as transformationally; that is, not to convey a content but to assist the hearer or reader to hope for or to achieve the same consciousness.[16]

Such irresolvable tension between experience and language, between what is felt and known and what is trying to make its way into words, is at the core of mystical literature and is quite present in the Spanish mystical writers. In the Prologue to the *Commentaries* on his own poem *Spiritual Canticle*, Saint John of the Cross offers what can be understood as a methodology of mystical writing:

> Because, who can write what to the amorous souls, where he dwells, he makes understand? And who can manifest with words the experience he makes them feel? And who, finally, what he makes them desire? Certainly, no one can! Certainly! Not even they [the souls] for whom it passes can. And this is the cause of why with figures, comparisons, and resemblances, they let overflow something from which they feel, and from the abundance of the spirit, they pour out mysterious secrets, that with reasons they declare.[17]

Following closely the Dionysian notion of mystical theology, Saint John of the Cross sets forth a method to commensurate experience and language: on the side of experience, he mentions the "understandings," "feelings," and "desires" acquired in the particular location of the encounter. On the side of language, he talks about the act of writing or "manifesting through words" "what they feel" and those "secret mysteries" that the soul attains. This means that the mystical writer finds that to translate the felt experience into a spatial-temporal language is to link the two through "figures, comparisons, and resemblances." He is implicitly comparing not only the experience with the language but also two

---

15 McGinn, xvii.
16 McGinn, xvii.
17 San Juan de la Cruz, *Cántico espiritual y Comentarios*, 10.

moments: the moment of the experience – not grounded in the limitations of time and space; and the moment in which the experience is described – the historical, recognizable moment of the act of writing.

Saint John of the Cross's method of mystical writing contains all the theoretical problems that have occupied and still occupy scholars of mysticism. Seemingly driven by an intellectual effort that resembles that of the mystics – to put into language an experience that does not adhere to words – scholars of mysticism (myself included) remain twice removed from the "truth" that mystics claim. Ours is a cerebral and imaginative exercise which nonetheless deserves attention for its perseverance, fruitful contradictions, comparative anxieties, and, in many cases, eccentricity. With this in mind, I will next examine the work of scholars which helped shape the ideas of mysticism of those who wrote about Spanish mystical literature inside and outside Spain.

1.1.1   *Philosophia Perennia*: William James

In most of the scholarship on Spanish mystical literature produced in the last century, we find the direct mention of William James's classic text *The Varieties of Religious Experience* (1902). A foundational twentieth-century scholar of mysticism, James was an earlier exponent of the theory of *Philosophia Perennia*, which proclaimed that a common denominator can be traced in mystical experiences across all religious and – according to James – non-religious practices that propel mystical states. In *The Varieties of Religious Experience*, James defines Perennialism in a nutshell:

> In Hinduism, in Neoplatonism, in Sufism, in Christian mysticism, in Whitmanism, we find the same recurring note, so that there is about mystical utterances an eternal unanimity which ought to make a critic stop and think, and which brings it about that the mystical classics have, as has been said, neither birthday nor native land.[18]

James's early Perennialism was marked by a psychological perspective. He speaks not of mysticism but of "mystical states of consciousness," which he describes with four qualities: the first two and the most pronounced features of mystical states are their ineffability and their noetic quality. The mystic declares that the experience "defies expression, that no adequate report of its contents can be given in words." Therefore, "its quality must be directly experienced," making the mystical more like states "of feeling than like states of intellect." While not intellectual, the mystical experience involves a "state of

---

18   William James, *The Varieties of Religious Experience*, 419.

knowledge" acquired through "illuminations" and "revelations."[19] The other two characteristics of mystical states, less prominent for James than their ineffability and noetic quality, are transiency – because they "cannot be sustained for long" – and passivity – because "the mystic feels as if his own will were in abeyance ... as if he were grasped and held by a superior power."[20]

Having established these four marks as the signs to trace in genuine mystical experiences, James posits that there are a "higher" and a "lower" mysticism.[21] Among the "higher" forms of mysticism, James cites the experiences recorded by the Spanish mystical writers, particularly the sixteenth-century mystics and writers Saint Teresa of Jesus and Saint John of the Cross. Within the "lower" forms of mysticism he includes states induced by effects of intoxicants such as drugs and alcohol. These are also "mystical," James argues, because "sobriety diminishes, discriminates, and says no, drunkenness expands, unites and says yes. It is in fact the great exciter of the Yes function in man."[22] But they are "lower" because "they open a region though they fail to give a map."[23]

To a modern scholar, James's ideas on mysticism, and in particular his statements about the Spanish mystics, could seem plainly broad-brushed. His writings appear at times too rushed to provide a context for experiences that he doesn't quite understand because of his linguistic and cultural distances from the mystics he writes about. For example, describing the prayer of union as explained in the works of Saint John of the Cross, James translates the Spanish noun *oración*, literally "prayer," as the archaic English term "orison" and thus refers to an "orison of union" to catalogue an experience that was different from prayer in general.[24] In commenting on the mystical ecstasies described in Saint Teresa of Jesus's writings, he writes that "for the medical mind," this is "hysteria," and "undoubtedly these pathological conditions have existed in many and possibly in all the cases" of mystical experiences.[25] To this, however, he adds that one should "pass a spiritual judgement upon these states, we must not content ourselves with superficial medical talk, but inquire into their fruits for life," whether or not they are also the fruits of hysteria.[26]

---

19   James, 380.
20   James, 380.
21   For James, the mystic's achievement is the overcoming of all the usual barriers between the individual and the Absolute (419), and this is commonly combined with pathological conditions of the person who experiences it.
22   William James, *The Varieties of Religious Experience*, 387.
23   James, 388.
24   James, 408.
25   James, 413.
26   James, 413.

James's outlook on Spanish mysticism also includes a nationalist discourse which will find a strong echo in the work of scholars to be discussed here. In commenting on a tendency to "stupefaction" and "helplessness" found in the French mystic Margaret Mary Alacoque, James writes:

> The otherworldliness encouraged by the mystical consciousness makes this over-abstraction from practical life peculiarly liable to befall mysticism ... but in natively strong minds and characters we find quite opposite results. The great Spanish mystics, who carried the habit of ecstasy as far as it has often been carried, appear for the most part to have shown indomitable spirit and energy, and all the more so for the trances in which they indulged.[27]

The contrast becomes evident between the "otherworldliness" of the French mystics and the "indomitable spirit and energy" of their Spanish comparands, who have the "habit of ecstasy." Such discourse has at its core an orientalist attitude toward Spain as separate and different from the rest of Europe. Such notions, as we will observe, dominated the scholarship on Spanish mysticism produced outside and inside Spain.[28]

Despite the vulnerability to criticism of our post-modern minds, James's scholarship was, and still is, foundational in providing a context and a language to write about mystical experience. Particularly valuable are his proposals to broaden the scope of mysticism beyond Christian frameworks and to establish a methodology of analysis for the study of the topic. Within the scholarship on Spanish mystical literature, we find James's work often cited, while also reframed according to specific cultural and political agendas. Scholars of Spanish mystical literature outside Spain – such as the Briton Edgar Allison Peers and the German Helmut Hatzfeld – and inside Spain, such as Ángel Cilveti, explicitly dialogue with James's Perennialism and psychological approaches in their analysis of Spanish mystical literature.

1.1.2   Evelyn Underhill: The Prominence of Christian Mysticism
Perennialist thought would take a different turn in the work of the widely-read English author Evelyn Underhill, often cited by Edgar Allison Peers in his works on Spanish mysticism. In her 1911 book *Mysticism: A Study in the Nature and Development of Man's Spiritual Consciousness*, Underhill contests James's psychological approach to mystical experiences. For her, mysticism is far from

---

27   James, 413.
28   This idea resonates with the "national characteristics of mystical language" described by Ángel Cilveti in the second half of the twentieth century, to be discussed here.

a peak experience, a form of "organic life" not to be equated with the effects of drugs as James does, or with any kind of extreme psychological state.[29] Underhill lists four fundamental qualities of mystics. First, mysticism is not lived as something passive and theoretical but active and practical. Second, the mystic is committed to a transcendental goal: "It is in no way concerned with adding on, exploring, re-arranging, or improving anything in the visible universe."[30] Third, God – whom Underhill describes as "the changeless One" – is for the mystic "never an object of exploration" but "a living and personal Object of Love." And lastly, the mystical state "is obtained neither from an intellectual realization of its delights nor from the most acute emotional longing" but by an arduous psychological and spiritual process, which Underhill further explores as "the Mystic Way." This "arduous" process that the mystic undergoes implies "the complete remaking of character and the liberation of a new, or rather latent, form of consciousness; which imposes on the self the condition ... called 'ecstasy.'"[31] Mysticism, Underhill insists, is not an opinion or a philosophy; and it is not to be identified with "religious queerness." Instead, it is "the name of that organic process which involves the perfect consummation of the Love of God."[32] These four qualities are the through-lines of Underhill's work, which she unfolds using examples from Christian and Catholic mystics, often citing Saint John of the Cross and, less often, Saint Teresa of Jesus.

Weighing these four qualities of mysticism that she defines, Underhill goes on to posit the superiority of Catholic Christian mysticism:

> Without prejudice to individual beliefs, and without offering an opinion as to the exclusive truth of any one religious system ... we are bound to allow as a historical fact that mysticism, so far, has found its best map on Christianity. Christian philosophy, especially that Neoplatonic theology which, taking up and harmonizing all that was best in the spiritual intuitions of Greece, India and Egypt, was developed by the great doctors of the early and mediaeval Church, supports and elucidates the revelations of the individual mystic as no other system of thought has been able to do.[33]

---

29   Evelyn Underhill, *Mysticism*, 90.
30   Underhill, 81.
31   Underhill explains further that she does not agree with the term "ecstasy," and renames it as a 'Unitive State.'
32   Underhill, *Mysticism*, 81.
33   Underhill, 104.

It is significant to notice here the language Underhill uses to declare the superiority of Western Christianity over all other mystical systems. She traces a map wherein Early Christianity is the "container" in which the knowledge of all religions – defined in geographical terms as Greece, India, and Egypt – has been distilled and imported to the West. Accordingly, Underhill continues, the "Christian atmosphere is the one in which the individual mystic has most often been able to develop his genius in a sane and fruitful way."[34] It is not only Christianity, though, but Catholicism where Underhill finds "the greatest mystics," the "Catholic saints."

Having established the superiority of Catholic Christian mysticism, Underhill acknowledges, with William James, the commonality of mystical experience across traditions: "'All mystics,' says Saint-Martin, 'speak the same language, for they come from the same country'" (80).[35] However, she insists on the need to not neglect the differences among traditions:

> Since mysticism is a form of life arising within every great religion, and tending towards essential Being, it is to be expected that all its manifestations should have some common characteristics. But since it shares the tendency to variation which is implicit in all life, we must also be prepared for genuine diversities, resulting not merely from race, climate or cultures, but from fundamental differences of spirit and outlook.[36]

Underhill's gesture of admitting the common traces of mystical experiences across traditions while declaring the superiority of Western Catholic Christianity is echoed in the work of other early-twentieth-century scholars such as Robert Charles Zaehner – also British, and one of the most cited scholars of mysticism. This is the case, too, with the majority of those who wrote about Spanish mystical literature inside and outside Spain, such as Miguel Asín Palacios, Edgar Allison Peers, Helmut Hatzfeld, and Ángel Cilveti.

1.1.3   From Mystical Experience to Mystical Language

The school of *Philosophia Perennia*, with its claim of the fundamental "sameness" of mystical experience across different religious traditions, was strongly criticized in the second half of the twentieth century, particularly in the United States. The 1978 collection of essays *Mysticism and Philosophical Analysis*, edited

---

34   Underhill, 105.
35   Here Underhill is citing a well-known phrase attributed to the French philosopher Louis-Claude de Saint-Martin.
36   Underhill, "Review," 485.

by Steven T. Katz, reacts to the "strong biases and problematic presuppositions" of Perennialist thought in favor of a philosophical and linguistic perspective as the most adequate means to examine mystical literature. Katz himself argues that there cannot be pure, unmediated mystical experience. Instead, each individual mystic is subjected to a pre-formed, anticipated experience conditioned by his or her culture, language, and other factors because "beliefs shape experience, just as experience shapes belief."[37]

Katz's ontological statement finds an echo in Carl A. Keller's approach to mystical literature. In the same volume, Keller presents a working definition of mystical literature as:

> [T]exts which deal with ultimate knowledge: with its nature, its modalities, its conditions, its methods, and also with secondary insights which might be granted to a seeker in the course of the pursue of his task.... Texts which discuss the path towards realization of the ultimate knowledge which each particular religion has to offer, and which contain statements about the nature of such knowledge.[38]

Having defined the qualities and varieties of mystical texts, Keller maintains that scholars should not take "these products of creative invention at their face value as expressions of personal mystical experience ... unless we postulate that poetical inspiration as such is identical with mystical experience."[39] Such a postulate, however, would be erroneous because inspiration does not equal mysticism, and mystical texts "do not necessarily reflect experience."[40] Nonetheless, Keller continues, the fact that mystical texts fail to reproduce the actual experience does not preclude their study. Mystical texts are a valuable source of analysis, given that scholars remain conscious of the boundaries between language and experience. Accordingly, "The study of mysticism is primarily, if not exclusively, a philological and an exegetical enterprise ... but scholarly work must be conscious of the gap which separates linguistic expression from experience."[41] Such a "gap" does not exclusively apply to the texts but also to the literary scholar or the theologian herself, whose own experience would not be commensurate with that of the writer:

---

37   Steven T. Katz, "Language, Epistemology, and Mysticism," 30.
38   Carl A. Keller, "Mystical Literature," 77.
39   Keller, 94.
40   Keller, 95.
41   Keller, 95.

> The aesthetic creed of modern rationalism is not the last word about truth ... but even if a theological approach is admitted, the student of mysticism cannot reach beyond his own personal experience.[42]

This call for an objective approach that separates mystical experience from the language of the texts into which the experience is poured – and which distinguishes clearly the experience of the scholar examining the mystical text from the experience of the mystical writer – would mark most of the scholarly work of mystical literature in the late twentieth century.

A different approach to the relation between mystical literature and mystical experience is found in the essay "Language and Mystical Awareness," by Frederick Streng, also published in *Mysticism and Philosophical Analysis* (1978). Streng calls scholars' attention to the importance of recognizing that mystical writers use language unconventionally. They "interpret the function of language differently."[43] According to Streng, mystical texts feature two functions of language, descriptive and transformative, which reveal different stages of mystical awareness of the writer. While descriptive language corresponds to the realm of forms and concepts, transformative language corresponds to a mode of awareness that is "more than, but inclusive of, intellect or ideas."[44] Paying very close attention to the mystical text, Streng maintains, it is possible to trace the "shift" between the descriptive or transformative functions of language, and, with that, the shift of awareness in the mystic writer. Accordingly, "the philosophical problem is how to understand the nature of the shift."[45] By focusing on the shift of language from descriptive to transformative, scholars may analyze the mystics' "effort either to reinforce or to avoid the attachment to terms, common assumptions about the descriptive function of concepts, or habitual expectations regarding the attributes of a class of things."[46] Streng's contribution to the discussion about experience and language – brilliant, in my opinion – is to establish the ability of language not to replicate the experience but to somehow bridge the distance between the experience and the particular context of the reader.

A similar approach to Streng's is found in modern scholars of mysticism such as Bernard McGinn – mentioned at the beginning of this volume – who have

---

42   Keller, 96.
43   Frederick Streng, "Language and Mystical Awareness," 142.
44   Streng, 143.
45   Streng, 144.
46   Streng, 152.

taken further the emphasis on the language of mystical texts. In his "Heuristic Sketch of Mysticism," McGinn confronts the overemphasis on experience by previous scholarship:

> Until recent years, overconcentration on the highly ambiguous notion of mystical experience has blocked careful analysis of the special hermeneutics of mystical texts, which have usually been treated without attention to genre, audience, structure, and even the simplest procedures for elucidating study of the text. Mystical masterpieces, which are often close to poetry in the ways in which they concentrate and alter language to achieve their ends, have all too often been treated like phone books or airline schedules: handy sources for confirming what we already expect.[47]

For McGinn, the question to ask from mystical texts is not that of experience. What mystical literature can teach us is not whether or not the author was a mystic according to our pre-conceived, and likely incomplete, notion of mystical experience. What we, scholars of mysticism, can coherently ask is: "What is the significance of her or his writings ... in the history of Christian mysticism?" and – we may add – in the history of all other religious traditions.

From the concentration on experience by the school of Perennialism to the focus on language, claimed by modern scholars like McGinn, we find the trajectory of the notion of mysticism as it has been understood in Western scholarship. In the case of the scholarship on Spanish mystical literature to be examined here, we will encounter a somehow parallel path, where early and mid-twentieth-century scholars, who were more focused on the question of origins, also understood mysticism in terms of experience. Towards the end of the twentieth and into the twenty-first century, we will observe a shift, still taking place, towards a concentration on the mystics' language, which while still subjective, scholars find more grounded than the notion of experience and open to dialogue with other traditions.

1.1.4   Michel De Certeau: Mystical Language and the Spanish Exception

Although the North American scholars discussed so far in this section have been rarely cited by scholarship on Spanish mysticism, their focus on language and on the performative aspect of the mystical texts became increasingly central to the study of Spanish mystics' writings in the late twentieth century, mainly through the influence of the French scholar Michel de Certeau – whose viewpoints both align and contrast with those of American scholars. De Certeau's

---

47   Bernard McGinn, *The Presence of God*, xiv.

well-known work *La Fable Mystique: XVIe–XVIIe siècle* brings into focus the creative tension between a mystical author's subject and the text she or he writes. De Certeau's core argument in this seminal work is that both – author and texts – share the state of being in transition. Accordingly, he explains that mystical writing begins with the factual contradiction of aiming to name that which cannot be named. Having established such a paradoxical intention, the mystic's speech becomes "a way of inquiry" which tends towards finding "the other in the text."[48] To do so, mystical speech deploys practices of *translation*, that is, mystical metaphors created by the author, who functions as a "translator" insofar as he or she is "a producer of otherness" by means of effecting linguistic displacement: "they [the mystic writers] attract words and change them."[49] From this conception of mystical speech as an act of translation and of mystical writers as those who translate between language and "otherness," it follows that the critical feature of mystical texts is not "what was said" but "how things were said."[50] For de Certeau, mystical language "loses the capacity to unveil: it veils. Its worth lies not in what it makes clear but in the operation it makes possible."[51] Michel de Certeau's concentration on language and "the operation it makes possible" marked a critical turning point in the scholarship on mystical literature, particularly in Europe. Late twentieth-century scholars of Spanish mysticism such as José Ángel Valente, one of the last authors whose work will be examined here, rely largely on de Certeau's semantic approaches.

However, some of de Certeau's underlying assumptions about the historical context of European mysticism deserve further examination. In his 1992 article "Mysticism" (co-authored by Marsanne Brammer), he posits a fair critique of Europeans' approach to Western and Eastern Mysticism: "The relationships that the European world maintained with itself and others had ... a determining role in the definition, the experience, and the analysis of mysticism."[52] De Certeau argues that in the sixteenth and seventeenth centuries, "European culture had ceased to define itself as Christian" and therefore the notion of mysticism detached itself from the institutional church. "Mysticism" was from then on not identified with any

> form of "wisdom" elevated by a full recognition of the mystery already lived and announced in common beliefs but rather an experimental

---

48   Michel de Certeau, *The Mystic Fable*, 5.
49   De Certeau, 119.
50   De Certeau, 164.
51   De Certeau, 147.
52   De Certeau and Brammer, "Mysticism," 13.

knowledge that slowly detached itself from traditional theology or church institutions.... In other words, what becomes mystical is that which diverges from normal or ordinary paths; that which is no longer inscribed within the social community of faith or religious reference, but on the margins of an increasingly secularized society and a knowledge that defines its own scientific objects.[53]

This new form of mysticism, developed in the margins of the secularized society, is characterized, according to de Certeau, "by the consciousness, received or acquired of a fulfilling passivity in which the self loses itself in God."[54]

What de Certeau does not consider either in this article or in the many references to the Spanish mystics in *La Fable Mystique* is that the secularization of Europe and the implied separation of mysticism from the institutional Church during the sixteenth and seventeenth centuries was not homogeneous for all of Europe. If the Europeans' quest for self-definition, which implied a geographical, linguistic, and religious practice of "othering" with respect to the rest of the world, determined the Western notion of mysticism, Spanish mysticism traversed a different path. In fact, for Spain, the sixteenth and the seventeenth centuries marked the opposite. Rather than ceasing to recognize itself as Christian – as the rest of Europe did, according to de Certeau – Spain was reasserting its Christianity and, in particular, its adherence to the Catholic Church. The most important Spanish mystics of the sixteenth century were not on the outskirts of the instructional church but right in its midst. And the "other" of Spain was not with respect to the rest of the world, but to itself.

1.2   Spanish Orientalism

De Certeau's omission of Spain's particularities in the process of European self-critique and its participation in the Western conception of the "mystic fable" resonates with Edward Said's acknowledged neglect of Spain in the orientalist map. In the prologue to the Spanish edition of his seminal work *Orientalism* (1994), Said confesses that he had only later realized that Spain was a "notable exception within the context of the general European model

---

53   De Certeau and Brammer, "Mysticism, "13.
54   The complete quotation reads: "In particular, from the time that European culture had ceased to define itself as Christian – that is, since the sixteenth or seventeenth century – one no longer designated as mystical that form of 'wisdom' elevated by a full recognition of the mystery already lived and announced in common beliefs but rather an experimental knowledge that slowly detached itself from traditional theology or church institutions, characterized by the consciousness, received or acquired of a fulfilling passivity in which the self loses itself in God." (De Certeau and Brammer, "Mysticism," 13.)

whose main features are described in *Orientalism*."⁵⁵ Both thinkers, either by generalization – as in de Certeau – or by focusing on certain national politics and languages – as in Said – disregarded the particular coordinates of one of the westernmost territories of Europe.⁵⁶

As mentioned earlier, the Spanish monarchy became a *monarchia universalis* in the late fifteenth century with the assistance of the Holy Office of the Inquisition. Together, the monarchy and the Inquisition ordered the capitulation, if not genocide, of all non-Christian subjects in 1492 – proceeding to the expulsion of the Jews from the Iberian Peninsula also in 1492 and of the Muslims in 1609. These "tectonic events," in the words of Gil Anidjar, marked the entry of Spain into Europe.⁵⁷ While Spain was reasserting its Christianity – not ceasing to recognize itself as Christian, as the rest of Europe was, according to de Certeau – it was doing so in constant tension with its internal "others," Jews and Muslims who remained in the peninsula. But the effort of the Monarchy, conversely, contributed to exacerbating the vision of Spain as "orientalist" throughout Europe.

As César Domínguez has demonstrated, in the nineteenth and early twentieth century, most European historians of literature used the term "orientalist" to describe Iberian/Spanish literature, "understood as the exaggeration of certain features of the southern geoliterary stratum where the peninsula lay …, and it was this positioning that accounted for the pronounced baroque nature of its literature."⁵⁸ The "oriental," Domínguez writes, is the term used by the rest of Europe to refer to Spain during this period, as well as the term used by Spain to talk about its internal "others":

---

55   Said, *Orientalism*, 9. For a detailed analysis of Said's position regarding Spain, see César Domínguez, "The South European Orient."
56   Post-colonial scholars such as Daniel Varisco (2007) have found in Said's frame of argument the essentialist mistake of stereotyping the West for the sake of de-stereotyping of the East, and of not mentioning the Orient for the sake of denouncing Orientalism. These could be the reasons for Said's neglect of Spain in the coordinates of an orientalist map. The case of de Certeau's omission is not strictly similar since he does rely on examples of Spanish mystics to construct his essential critical work of *The Mystic Fable*. Still, the inaccuracy of his historical references to Saint John of the Cross and other Spanish literary sources, as well as his somehow forceful arguments about the Spanish mystics, show that de Certeau's focus was in great measure concentrated on his own linguistic project. The work of this renowned theorist would have benefitted from a more thorough investigation into the historical circumstances of Spain.
57   Gil Anidjar, "Jewish Mysticism Alterable and Unalterable," 125.
58   César Domínguez, "The South European Orient," 425. Here Domínguez is commenting upon ideas from the work of Friedrich Bouterwak, Jean Charles Léonard de Sismondi and Friedrich Schlegel.

In this regard, the relationship of the Iberian Peninsula to orientalist narratives is paradoxical, as its supposed orientalist otherness came from within and without: while the rest of Europe created an orientalist image of the peninsula, the Iberian community used orientalism as a means to define *internal* others in the gypsy territory of Andalusia.[59]

This European vision of Iberia as oriental explains to a certain extent de Certeau's detour from the specificities of Iberia as well as Said's non-realization of Spain's particular situation in the mapping of orientalism. Likewise, the scholarly works on Spanish mystical literature that we will examine in the following pages, whether written by Spaniards or non-Spaniards, are circumscribed – explicitly or implicitly – within the context of the internal and external orientalist dynamics that Domínguez describes.

One of the most relevant Spanish historians of the twentieth century, Américo Castro – well known for his work attempting to balance out what Domínguez calls internal and external orientalism – wrote in a letter to the Spanish writer Juan Goytisolo: "The truth is that these unfortunate people were never told who they were, or the reasons why they were who they were."[60] This self-unawareness denotes the internal forms of orientalism. As Goytisolo points out later in his commentaries to Castro's letters, becomes obvious in the absence of Jews and Muslims in the most common references to Peninsular literature:

> Castilian literature was examined – and unfortunately it is still being examined by some thoughtful heads curiously impermeable to the language of facts – as a function of Latin-Christian coordinates, accepting at most a casual Arabic and Jewish contagion.[61]

The intellectual exercise of examining Castilian literature as exclusively dependent upon Latin Christianity is a manifestation of the phenomenon of inside orientalism practiced by national scholars. Here, Goytisolo – commenting on Castro's letters – may have had in mind scholars such as Dámaso Alonso, to whom we will soon refer, whose "Italian thesis" attempted to establish an exclusive Roman and Italian influence in the work of Saint John of the

---

59 Domínguez, 427.
60 *El epistolario (1968–1972): Cartas de Américo Castro y Juan Goytisolo*, Escudero Rodríguez, Javier, ed., 136.
61 *El epistolario (1968–1972): Cartas de Américo Castro a Juan Goytisolo*, Javier Escudero Rodríguez, ed., 13.

Cross, an idea consonant with the history that was being constructed by the National-Catholic ideology during or leading up to the Francoist dictatorship (1936–1975).

For most Spanish intellectuals, their national mystical literature is a difficult topic precisely because of the "orientalist" qualities they encounter in it. Thus, their effort is in many cases directed to assert the Christian and European character of Spanish mystical literature by contraposing it with everything "oriental." With this, they manage to reclaim their national mystical wealth while at the same time defending it from orientalist valorizations coming from the outside. But that is not the only orientalist quality of the scholarship on Spanish mystical literature.

One of the key features of orientalism, as Edward Said puts it, is a sense of "eternal temporality," meant to create the impression of repetition and force but with the secondary effect of a diminishing valorization.[62] In the scholarly work on Spanish mystical literature produced inside and outside Spain up to the second half of the twentieth century, we find a similar sense of "eternal temporality." This scholarship is mostly permeated by a sort of intellectual bewilderment which, in turn, creates an excess of non-referentiality and inaccessibility which ultimately annuls the mystical text, an effect equivalent to the diminishing valorization of orientalism that Said notices. As we will soon observe, this attitude of passive criticism was justified by prominent national scholars as their inability to access the experience that the texts claim and, therefore, their lack of means for judging the literature born from such experience. However, behind this quasi-religious imperative lies the same political and political agenda that promotes the displacement of everything oriental from Spain. As a result, both mystical literature and the very notion of the oriental remain in the outskirts of critical analysis.

The notions of orientalism and mysticism, along with their complicated intricacies in the context of Spain, will serve as a framework for our critical analysis in the remainder of this volume.

2   The Scholarship on Spanish Mystical Literature Pre-1942

2.1   *Marcelino Menéndez Pelayo and the Terror of the Orient*

One of the first Spanish scholars to place mystical literature under the egis of literary criticism was Marcelino Menéndez Pelayo. In his lecture at his induction into the Royal Academy of the Spanish Language in 1881, published later

---

62   Edward Said, *Orientalism*, 92.

under the title "La poesía mística en España," this prominent academician chose to address the topic of Spanish mysticism, "pleasant to all Christian and Spanish souls."[63] His discourse consisted of an evaluation of Spanish mystical literature, placing particular stress on establishing what is within and what is outside its scope. Menéndez Pelayo opened his speech with a broad definition of mystical poetry as a "translation in the form of art of all the theologies and philosophies animated by a personal and living feeling of the poet who sings to his spiritual loves."[64] To this ample description he added: "Mystical poetry is not synonymous with Christian poetry; it encompasses more and less."[65] Such a "more and less" measure became the main category deployed by Menéndez Pelayo throughout his speech. Within the "more," he identified the mystical literature produced by Catholic Christians; and within the "less" category, he placed the writings of non-Christian mystics, which he specifically located within the domain of the oriental.[66]

Reading Menéndez Pelayo's speech carefully, one realizes that his notions of Spanish mystical poetry, and of mysticism in general, are strictly correlated with his stances on what he calls "the Orient." For him, Christianity is identified with the Western world – whose roots he firmly locates in the ancient Greek and Roman civilizations – while the non-Christian is identified with the oriental. Within this taxonomy, Menéndez Pelayo deploys ample rhetorical skills to argue that the philogenetic birth of Spanish culture is to be found in the Christian-Roman tradition. Accordingly, Spanish mystical literature is within the "more" because it is Christian:

> [O]nly in Christianity does this poetry live perfectly and purely.... Beyond the humanized Christ, ... which art, which sacred poetry could exist that is not monstrous like the Indian or solitary and infertile like that of the Hebrews from the Middle Age?[67]

Objectionable terms such as the Indian "monstrosity," the Hebrew "infertility," and what Menéndez Pelayo labels as the "excessively refractory nature of

---

63 Marcelino Menéndez Pelayo, "La poesía mística en España," In *La mística española*, ed. Pedro Sáinz Rodríguez (Madrid: Editorial Afrodisio-Aguado, 1956), 6.
64 Menéndez Pelayo, 6.
65 Menéndez Pelayo, 7.
66 This distinction between the "more" and "less" mystical resonates with William James's later qualification of higher and lower mysticisms. Although the contexts of discussion differ, one can observe in both scholars the tendency to taxonomize the category of mysticism.
67 Menéndez Pelayo, "La poesía mística," 9.

the Arabic race" effect a radical denial of the literary influence of Arabic and Hebrew authors in Spanish literature.[68]

There are moments in his discourse "La poesía mística" when Menéndez Pelayo seems unable to deny the "mysticism" of non-Christian authors. For example, within the category of "less" mysticism, he reluctantly includes the Iberian Jewish poet Ibn Gabirol (Yehudah Ibn Gabirol) as an example of an author who, while not a Christian, is still a mystic thanks to the influence of the Roman Empire in Jewish philosophy. He praises Ibn Gabirol's poetry as "resplendent," but such a complement is short-lived, as he immediately describes his prose as "pessimist and deliriant."[69] Likewise, he insists on denying any direct influence of Ibn Gabirol on Christian mystical literature because "When, from shadows, did light appear?" But placing a Jewish mystic within the "less" mystical category is more than what Menéndez Pelayo does for the Muslim poets. He suggests that the same Hellenistic "sparks" that helped Jewish poetry attain the status of mysticism "reached the Arabs, even though they are the most resistant race to intellectual speculation and to the meditation of divine matters. Not even one mystical verse do I find in all that has been translated of their poets."[70] Similar expressions are found throughout his historiographical incursions to link the birth of the Spanish nation to the Roman Empire while denying or plainly rejecting any trace of "oriental," and particularly Arabic, influence on Spanish mystical literature. For Menéndez Pelayo, the "oriental" had the effect of obscuring the purity of the ancient Romans, a space in which he – like many of his countrymen would do following the hegemonic discourse of National-Catholicism – located the birth of Spanish culture.

In only one instance does Menéndez Pelayo use the word "oriental" to refer to an author whom he judges to be the peak of Spanish mysticism: Saint John of the Cross. The point of contention is that Menéndez Pelayo finds no way to bypass the influence of the Biblical Hebrew epithalamium the Song of Songs in Saint John of the Cross's poetry. The Song of Songs is at the very core of the formation of both Christian and Hebrew mysticism.[71] As McGinn reminds

---

68 Menéndez Pelayo, 8.
69 Menéndez Pelayo, 23.
70 Menéndez Pelayo, 21.
71 The recognition of the Song of Songs' influence on the work of the Spanish mystics is even more complicated if one considers that the Council of Trent (1546) maintained the prohibition against the translation of the Bible into vernacular languages; and this recalls the famous Inquisitorial case against Fray Luis de León, professor at the University of Salamanca while Saint John of the Cross was a student there, for privately translating the Song of Songs into Spanish. Menéndez Pelayo's contradiction appears then not as a fruit of his own but as an inherited problem between the orientalism of the Hebrew canonical texts as part of the Christian canon and the Romanization of Christian Iberia.

us, to neglect the Jewish roots of Christian mysticism and to see it as a purely Greek phenomenon is to risk misconstruing an important part of its history.[72] But this is not what Menéndez Pelayo intended. He does acknowledge the link between the most important Spanish mystic poet and the Song of Songs. However, in doing so, he immediately withdraws from inquiry and falls into a sort of religious dread: "This oriental poetry, transplanted from the tops of the Mount Carmel and the flowered valleys of Zion.... I confess that they [John of the Cross' poems] instill religious terror when I touch them."[73] "Religious terror" was Menéndez Pelayo's reaction to the undeniable presence of the oriental in the mystical writings of one of the most important Spanish poets and a Catholic saint.

In the following pages, we will find that Menéndez Pelayo's "religious terror" would become a motif throughout the scholarship on Spanish mystical literature – particularly on Saint John of the Cross's work – produced in Spain during the first half of the twentieth century. This "syndrome of terror," as José Ángel Valente named it, resulted from the inside orientalist narrative that had been reinforced in the Peninsula by the political and religious agenda of the Franco regime.[74] It is, moreover, a sign of the adherence to the prevalent ideology that defined the language used to talk about Spanish mystical literature until the post-Franco era.

2.2 Miguel Asín Palacios: Mysticism, Orientalism, and Comparison

Not all Spanish scholars of mystical literature adopted the same position vis-a-vis the internal/external dynamics of orientalism in Spain. A very different approach from that of Menéndez Pelayo is found in the work of one of the most controversial Spanish scholars of the early twentieth century and father of the studies of comparative religion in Spain, Miguel Asín Palacios. Asín Palacios was a Roman Catholic priest, professor of Arabic at the Universidad Central de Madrid, now Complutense, founder of the first Spanish orientalist academic journal, *Al-Andalus* (along with his teacher Julián Rivera and his student Emilio Garcia Gómez, both renowned Arabists), and president of the Royal Academy of Spanish Language until his death in 1944. He gave rise, in the words of Maria Rosa Menocal, to "one of the more far-reaching schools of revisionist thought about the Arabic question in Spain."[75]

---

72 Bernard McGinn, *The Foundations of Mysticism: Origins to the Fifth Century*, 22.
73 Menéndez Pelayo, "La poesía mística," 48.
74 José Ángel Valente, "Formas de lectura y dinámica de la tradición." In *Hermenéutica y mística: San Juan de la Cruz*, ed. José Ángel Valente and José Lara Garrido (Madrid: Editorial Tecnos, 1995), 16.
75 Maria Rosa Menocal, Review of *Don Miguel Asín Palacios*, 260.

In Asín Palacios's writings, we perceive the struggle to find a middle way between the internal and external orientalist practices, and to reconcile his profound admiration for the Sufis with his strong commitment to Christian Catholic beliefs. His prolific scholarship focused on two aspects: religion and language, in particular, mysticism and Arabic, the language used by the Sufis, the mystics of Islam. He saw the need for Spanish academia to develop orientalist studies, and with them, comparative studies. Despite all his biases, Asín Palacios's comparative work is rigorous for his and our own time. In it, we find a scholar concerned with adherence to objective logic, sometimes in tension with a rather conservative Catholic priest who, in order to attest the superiority of Christianity, would make affirmations that today would be aptly criticized, such as this one: "The Sufis are pleased to cite at each step decrees of the highest perfection, attributed to Jesus … in order to fill the vacuum that they find in the Qur'an…. They were forced to vivify their dead writings with the spirit of Christian examples."[76]

While today's comparative scholars, educated as we are in the post-orientalist era, would be less than welcoming to such an affirmation, Asín Palacios's foundational scholarship is key to the trajectory of scholarship on Spanish mystical literature produced in Spain during the twentieth century. Accordingly, I will be closely examining Asín Palacios's work, asking questions which are relevant to today's scholars such as: How did Asín Palacios design his comparative project? What were his key premises and questions? What metaphors did he use to illustrate his comparative methodology? How did he solve the tension between the boundaries of his Christian Catholic religious commitment and what he found admirable and worthy of study in Islam? How did he deal with the "anxiety of influence" of the Spanish academia when comparing Christian mystics and Sufi authors?

2.2.1   A Historical Approach

The central question in Asín Palacios' work is historical: where and what is the hidden connection that explains the poetic and the theological parallels between medieval Hispano-Arab Sufis and sixteenth-century Spanish Christian mystics? In responding to this historical inquiry, Asín Palacios sought to solve a religious and a theological dilemma: why are the writings of Spanish mystics and of Hispano-Arab Sufis so alike? His fundamental response to his own question was that such a connection, which he depicts as "broken stitch point," was to be found in early Christian monasticism. Asín Palacios's query and argument are at the core of the dynamics of inside and outside orientalism

---

76   Asín Palacios, *El Islam cristianizado*, 8–9.

at play in the scholarship on Spanish mysticism in the early twentieth century. They are also in a close although implicit dialogue with contemporary scholarship on mysticism and religion in Western scholarship.

At first sight, Asín Palacios seems to be establishing a dialogue with the school of *Philosophia Perennia*. In a move similar to, but with different outcomes from that of William James and Evelyn Underhill, the Spanish scholar asks:

> Was there in Islam a proper mystic life, that is, with features at least similar to those shown in the Christian mystic life? What is the cause of such similarities? What historical origin could sufficiently explain the reason of their [the similarities'] existence? Is this a merely verbal and formal analogy, or does it transcend into the essence of spiritual life and thought?[77]

With these words, Asín Palacios echoes James's psychological language as well as Underhill's assertion that mysticism finds "its best map in Christianity."[78] But the Spanish scholar also breaks from the Perennialists by focusing on the question on influences and approaching it from a historical perspective.

That for Asín Palacios the thesis of an essential similarity in the experience of all mystics wasn't enough to explain the commonalities which he discovered between Christian Carmelite and Sufi mysticism becomes evident at the beginning of his *El Islam cristianizado*:

> From the start, we should refuse the hypothesis of a mere casual coincidence. These analogies are too typical and too many to be the result of just an identity of ideas and religious feelings common to the bottom of human psychology.... This is an organic set of problems whose solution is of interest to the historian of religions as well as to the theologian. Therefore, such a solution should be searched for in the light of theology and history. That is, observing the facts and considering the principles so that, if possible, they may be harmonized.[79]

Thus focused on the historical-theological quest, Asín Palacios's scholarship – like many of his contemporaries' work – is permeated by a kind of "an anxiety

---

77 Asín Palacios, *El Islam cristianizado*, 8–9.
78 Underhill, *Mysticism*, 104.
79 Asín Palacios, *El Islam cristianizado*, 9.

of influence."[80] But unlike his contemporaries, Asín Palacios advanced a methodology of comparison for mystical texts from which, in spite of all its flaws, modern scholars can learn much.

2.2.2 Comparison by Analogy

The "anxiety of influence" manifests in Asín Palacios's work from the moment he refuses the use of the very term "influence." In his article "Un precursor musulmán de San Juan de la Cruz" ("A Muslim precursor of Saint John of the Cross") Asín writes:

> The very word influence brings to the mind the idea of copy or imitation, suggesting ineptitude or poor inventiveness in that one who copies. Therefore, we reject it [the term "influence"] instinctively when applied to ourselves or to something that we care for.[81]

In order to avoid mention of an "influence," Asín Palacios advances a method of comparison that he describes as "analogy": "Two elements which are analogous to a third element from which both proceed, should be analogous to each other."[82] The syllogism of this comparative approach is that two elements (Christian mysticism and Sufism) which are each analogous to a third element (early Oriental Christianity), must therefore be analogous to themselves. In other words, if the sixteenth-century Spanish Christian mystics sought to imitate their early founders (the Oriental Christians), and the Sufis did the same, knowingly or unknowingly, then it can be reasoned that Christian mystics and Sufis share a common ground that makes them "analogous" to each other.

Asín Palacios's analogical method serves him to not only explain the literary and theological coincidences found in the writings of Spanish Christian mystics and Sufis but also to make the radical religious claim that Sufis were "Christians without knowing it," all the while avoiding the reference to a direct influence and establishing the pre-eminence of Christianity:

> It is evident that the Sufis or mystic Muslims speak and act, in many cases, exactly like the Christian mystics. Excluding the dogmas of the Trinity and of the Holy Incarnation – and therefore of the divinity of Christ – the

---

80 Here, I am using Harold Bloom's coined phrase in its more general meaning of an apprehension regarding the matter of literary sources.
81 Asín Palacios, "Un precursor musulmán de San Juan de la Cruz," *Al-Andalus*, no. 1 (1933), 32.
82 Asín Palacios, *El Islam cristianizado*, 14.

theological ideas, ascetic methods, and mystical theories, are completely analogous. It is true that the exclusion of these dogmas … makes quite difficult [for Sufi mystics] the indispensable psychological process needed to conceive and to experiment the highest degrees of spiritual life.[83]

Deploying the analogical method as the basis for his comparison, Asín Palacios created – as most comparativists do – comparative metaphors that illustrate his thought process. Among his comparative metaphors, we find "two harmonized echoes of the same far-away voice" and "two symmetrical images of the same object reflected in two distinct mirrors." These two metaphors appear often in the Spanish scholar's writing to support his thesis that it was possible to draw a historical and theological continuum between the Sufi and the Christian Carmelite tradition not because there was a direct influence between the two but because both shared the "common trunk" of Oriental Christian Monasticism.

2.2.3 The New Disciplines of Comparative Philology and Comparative Religion

Asín Palacios's method of "comparison by analogy" involved two fields of study that were relatively new for early twentieth-century Europe, and groundbreaking for Spanish academia: comparative philology – which he calls "comparative literature" – and comparative religion, which he terms "comparative theology." His analogical comparative method, as he first presented it in *El Islam cristianizado*, supports his argument that the most important Hispano-Arabic Sufi of the 13th century, Ibn 'Arabi, was actually "a Christian" because although his "spiritual teachings and methods … essentially coincide with Islamic traditions," they have a "profound Christian character."[84] To support his thesis, Asín Palacios relied on comparative philology and comparative religion, becoming one of the first scholars in Spain to deploy linguistics as a bridge to compare not just religions but theologies:

> Where this lexical comparison promises surprising results is, without a doubt, in Muslim ascetic mysticism … the analytical study of Sufi terms compared with the Oriental and Western Christian monasticism…. I believe I can demonstrate that Sufi technical terminology, a true nightmare of research because of its mysterious sense, is nothing but the

---

83 Asín Palacios, *El Islam cristianizado*, 14.
84 Asín Palacios, 269.

imitation of a procedure followed by the first eremites among the Egyptian Christian monastics.[85]

Accordingly, Asín Palacios implemented comparative philology by resorting to a series of linguistic traces in the main theological terms and poetic imagery used by Ibn ʿArabi and Saint John of the Cross. And he used comparative theology by posing the argument that Hispano-Arab Sufis are part of the "soul of the Catholic Church" although not of its "body" because their foundations are in primitive oriental Christianity.

Although Asín Palacios was the first to develop comparative philology and comparative religion in Spain, he was not completely original. Rather, he was trying to come to terms with the nineteenth-century European "discovery" of the world religions and its consequent mapping of the world according to the new linguistic and religious coordinates. The process of development of these two disciplines is critical to understanding Asín Palacios's claims and scholarship on Spanish mystical literature in general. The scholarly field of religion, as Tomoko Masuzawa has noticed, can be understood as a product of the parallel emerging science of language.[86] Comparative philology and comparative religion impacted the linguistic and geopolitical remapping of Europe, the Middle East, and Asia during the nineteenth century, a period when Spain came to be known by the rest of Europe as an oriental territory. And consequently, these studies played an important role in the re-organization of the world religions that took place by the beginning of the twentieth century – when Spain came to be seen as a unique, "mystical" land – assuming a mutual imbrication between the categories of the "oriental" and the "mystical."

The European school of comparative philology was fueled by the "discovery" of the Sanskrit language during the British colonization of India in the eighteenth century. Sanskrit attracted the attention of European philologists due to its linguistic and semantic complexity. It soon began to be compared with Greek and Latin, becoming a third classical language and giving rise to the discipline of comparative philology, also known in its beginnings as comparative linguistics.[87] One goal of comparative linguists was to find "the original

---

85   Asín Palacios, 35–36.
86   Tomoko Masuzawa, *The Invention of World Religions*, 209.
87   Early in his career, Asín Palacios studied Sanskrit at the Universidad Central de Madrid. While it was unlikely that he was attracted to the Sanskrit language with the intention of continuing Hinduism studies, he did it because the language was deemed indispensable for understanding the origin of religions. Thus, his incursion in Sanskrit was an incursion in comparative philology and comparative religion. His Sanskrit professor, Francisco Ayuso, was the first Spanish scholar known to study Sanskrit outside Spain. Ayuso's

language," which now seemed to be situated further East. They were also tasked with organizing the newly-discovered languages into Aryan (Indo-European) and Semitic (Hebrew and Arabic). This division of languages, Masuzawa reminds us, "facilitated a new expression of Europe's age-old animosity toward the Islamic powers, insofar as this science categorized Jews and Arabs as being 'of the same stock,' conjointly epitomizing the character of the Semitic race."[88] In the first decades of the twentieth century, when Asín Palacios had finished his doctoral studies and was working on the manuscript of *Islam Cristianizado*, European linguists devoted to comparative philology, such as Martin Haug and Max Müller, started inquiring into parallel analyses of comparative linguistics and religion. These studies brought about the new discipline of comparative religion, which was in charge of making sense of the religious traditions related to the newly-discovered languages. Just as the family of Greco-Latin languages was substituted for the family of Indo-European languages, the world religions were re-organized as Aryan, Indo-European, and Semitic – this last group containing Hebrew and Arabic.

The European scholars contemporary with Asín Palacios were theologians who practiced comparative philology and comparative religion. Among them, one finds the young Spanish comparativist in implicit conversation with the German Otto Pfleiderer, who, in a series of lectures given in Berlin and published in an English translation as *Religion and Historic Faith* (1906), argued that Sufism had an Aryan origin. Pfleiderer maintained that Sufism is not the product of Islam, although framed by it, and that "it must remain undecided whether it owes its origin to ancient Persian, Indian or Neo-platonic Gnosticism."[89] This view of Sufism as being Aryan can be interpreted, as Masuzawa does, as envisioning a future world-Christianity held by early nineteenth-century comparativists. Although his name does not appear in the studies of early comparative philology and religion (like Masuzawa's work cited here), Asín Palacios's ideas are in dialogue with Pfleiderer's proposal of the Aryan origins of Sufism. The main difference is that Asín Palacios attributes to Sufism a direct Christian input that Pfleiderer did not consider.

---

teacher was the German Martin Haug, one of the pioneers of comparative philology and comparative religion. Later on, in 1899, Asín Palacios taught a course on world religions, including Hinduism and Buddhism, at the Conciliar Seminary of Zaragoza. We now know that his World Religions course included comparative topics because in his *Manual of World Religions*, Asín Palacios writes down his own comments on topics such as *nirvana* and yoga, and compares them with Christian traditions. (See: *Miguel Asín Palacios: Estudiante de lengua sánscrita y profesor de la filosofía religiosa de la India*. López Baralt, Luce, and Gloria Maité Hernández, eds. Madrid: Mandala Ediciones, 2015.)

88   Masuzawa, 26.
89   Otto Pfleiderer, *Religion and Historic Faiths*, trans. Daniel A. Huebsch, New York: B. W. Heubsch, 1907, quoted in Masuzawa, 202.

2.2.4   Asín Palacio's Internal and External Orientalisms

Although rarely discussed outside Spanish-speaking academia, the implicit dialogue of Asín Palacios with the European "new sensitivity of global awareness" was radical for his time. Asín Palacios was well aware of the ideas of his European contemporaries and that he was conversing with them from his own position within the Spanish academy.[90] Regarded by his own Spaniard colleagues in quite ambivalent terms, the scholarship of Asín Palacios shook the geopolitical image of orientalism and mysticism in Spain. As already explained, while other European nations were waking up to a global consciousness, Spain was still recovering from the Napoleonic invasion (1808–1813) and immersed in its own post-colonial crisis. Therefore, other countries, mainly France and Germany, were noticing in Spain not a global awareness but the evidence of an oriental European space. As César Domínguez has noticed, the European-spread vision of Spain at the turn of the century was that of an eternal, oriental, mystical territory where the Semitic languages of Hebrew and Arabic were beautifully mixed with the "national" Spanish, and the Christian religion was mixed with the Eastern faiths.[91] This vision conceives of Iberia as a bridge between Europe and Africa, East and West, Christianity and Islam. But the image of a bridge – Domínguez suggests – renders Spain impossible to homogenize because a bridge is always between things, neither on one side nor on the other. Within this context, Asín Palacios's comparative scholarship was storming that bridge by arguing not for a homogenization but a historical continuum. His comparative analogical argument aimed to expand the Spanish Christian geo-religious map instead of intersecting it:

> Because it is not valueless for the history of Spanish and European religious thought, the fact, to many unknown, that in the same land of those [Saint Teresa of Jesus and Saint John of the Cross] flourished, three centuries before, a Muslim mystic who, despite his theological prejudices, would hold latent in the depths of his subconsciousness the guiding light of Christian spirituality, capable of dictating to him morals and precautions so similar to those that the Carmelite school would later formulate.[92]

These words can be understood as an attempt to neutralize the image of Spain as endlessly oriental and mystical by fulfilling a historical and religious agenda, somehow similar to that of Ramón Menéndez Pidal but still quite

---

90   Asín Palacios attended the congresses of Orientalists in Argel and Copenhagen (1905 and 1908) and his work was much commented on by European and North American scholars.
91   Domínguez, "The South European Other," 426.
92   Asín Palacios, *El Islam Cristianizado*, 269.

distinct. Affirming that the Sufis were "Christians without knowing it" because Christianity and Islam shared the common grounds of oriental Christianity; and arguing – calling upon no other than Thomas Aquinas – that Sufis were part of the soul of the Catholic Church although not of its body, Asín Palacios was bringing home, to Christian terms, all that he found worthy in Sufism and Islam.[93] With this, he managed to reverse the orientalist map of early twentieth-century Europe not by guarding it from Muslims, and therefore neutralizing its oriental halo, but by incorporating them into the Spanish linguistic and Christian religious historical continuum. The Christianization of Islam, was for him also its "Hispanization."

Asín Palacios's attempt to adopt the inside other by Christianizing it may seem rather colonial to us. From our twenty-first century, post-orientalist perspective, his comparative practices can be interpreted as a crusade-like Christianization of Islam, and as a Hispanization of the Arabic language, even as a scholarly act of conversion. However, for Asín Palacios's time, this was a courageous, if also eccentric, comparative gesture. He took the category of mysticism beyond its Christocentric context by noticing that mystics of other religions also attain high spiritual stages. If the Sufis, being the heart of true Islamic religion, were nothing else than Christians without knowing it, then Muslims can be equal to "genuine" Christians. Accordingly, in Asín Palacios's work there is an implicit acknowledgement that the Orient is within Spain, not outside of it. His comparison is not between internal Western Christianity and external Eastern Islam, but between internal Christianity and internal Islam. Asín Palacios's act of comparison, grounded in terms of philological and theological comparative disciplines, had a tremendous impact on the future of the scholarship on Spanish mystical literature, particularly in the work of Luce López-Baralt, to be examined later in this volume.

2.3 *The External Orientalism of Edgar Allison Peers*

The orientalist attitude of the rest of Europe toward the Iberian Peninsula was in great part initiated by England in the context of the Anglo-Spanish War (1585–1604).[94] Barbara Fuchs has demonstrated that from the end of the

---

93   It is important to notice that in *La escatología musulmana en la Divina Comedia* (1919), Asín Palacios proposes rather an Islamization of Dante, the prominent figure of the European Renaissance. As well, in the posthoumous *Sadilíes y Alumbrados* (1989), his position again varies from the one maintained in *Islam cristianizado*.

94   This was a sporadic series of battles that started with the English attack on Spanish Netherlands and ended with an agreement to cease military interventions. In 1588, the British army defeated the *Armada Invencible* (Spanish Armada) of the Spanish King Phillip II, who attempted to take over British territory and expand his Empire towards

sixteenth and far into the nineteenth and twentieth centuries, British promoted an image of Spain as England's other both racially – as the "colored" oriental – and religiously – as Catholic. This attitude of racial othering is obvious in the use of terms such as "Moorish" or "Turkish," commonly used in English literature of the period to refer to Spaniards. Such terms denote – as Fuchs remarks – a "powerful early form of orientalism that disregards actual geographic or religious borders to emphasize the alterity of England's most powerful enemy."[95] Religiously, England depicted Spain as buried in the dark shadow of the Catholic Church. While the Reformation of England created a considerable migration of Catholics to Spain, Protestant England built its religious identity by perpetuating the opposition between the British Anglican and the Spanish Catholic churches. Although this religious picture of Spain as ultra-Catholic promoted by England was not in total disagreement with the Spanish Empire's view of itself, that was not the case with the racial othering. The racial image of Spain as "oriental," mainly Muslim, contrasted with the identity that the Spanish monarchy has strongly predicated since the fifteenth century – that of having a Roman-Christian past that was free of Jewish and Muslim influences. Such tension between the English vision of Spain and the Spanish vision of itself was alive far into the nineteenth century. David Howarth notices that the English "invention" of Spain, was not just a political strategy involving the circles of power but an enterprise involving the arts, the literature, and mainly the religious discourses. In Howarth's words, "the interest of the British in Spanish religiosity was morbid, inseparable from the fears men had as to the reappearance of a proscribed faith in Britain."[96] The British not only failed to understand the Iberian Peninsula on its own terms, but also misunderstood it and projected that erroneous image of Spain into the rest of Europe and the English-speaking world.

Much of this "morbid" interest in Spanish religiosity is evident in the work of the British scholar Edgar Allison Peers (1891–1952), pioneer of English Hispanic Studies and the first to introduce Spanish mystical literature to English-speaking readers.[97] In 1924, Peers published his *Spanish Mysticism: A Preliminary Survey*, with the purpose of showing the world the richness of

---

northern Europe. This was the most disastrous defeat for the Spanish Empire during the Anglo-Spanish war.

95   Fuchs, "Sketches of Spain: Early Modern England's 'Orientalizing' of Iberia," 64.
96   Howarth, *The Invention of Spain*, xi.
97   In the Introduction to a 1997 collection of essays honoring Peers published by Liverpool University, where he taught, his academic personality is depicted as "having a pragmatic cast of mind and a deep sensuality, he held strong religious convictions (he was a devout high Anglican and lay preacher) which predisposed him toward the mystical."

Spanish mystical literature, which, in his own words, had "not yet been fully realized" even by Spanish people. This publication was followed by his two-volume *Studies of the Spanish Mystics* in 1927 and by his English translations of the works of Raymond Llull (1923), John of the Cross (1942, 1953), and Teresa of Jesus (1946). His biography of John of the Cross, entitled *Spirit of Flame*, was published in New York in 1944, and became the first book that Americans read about the Spanish mystic.[98]

Peers begins the first chapter of his *Spanish Mysticism*, entitled "España Mística," with an observation that speaks of the orientalist lens through which he looked at Spain:

> No thoughtful traveler can spend many weeks in Spain without perceiving that mysticism is inborn in its people.... Nor can he for long be content to look upon the Spain of legend – of the "black legend" which has done so much in our own land to obscure the greatness of this country which is its victim.[99]

The innate quality of mysticism in the Spanish character becomes the driving motif throughout Peers's scholarship on Spanish mystical literature. But Peers's goal is not to reinforce the British image of Spain as oriental and buried in the darkness of an outdated Catholicism. Rather, he aims to correct this error by showing that Spain is not the land of the "black legend." Instead of a religious, impoverished Spain, Peers seeks to showcase an "age-long devotion to an ideal," that of a "Greater Spain, – for the Cross."[100] Peers goes on to argue throughout his book that mystical literature appeared in sixteenth-century Spain all of a sudden, as a spontaneous impulse; and that mysticism is, for reasons he does not quite explain, inherent to the Spanish people.[101] Peers's mode of external orientalism is, then, a curious case. On one hand, he assumes a militant language akin to that of early twentieth-century Spanish intellectuals

---

(Anne L. Mackenzie, ed. *Spain and its Literature: Essays in Memory of E. Allison Peers* (London: Liverpool University Press, 1997), 27.)

98 In 1958, the biography of Juan de la Cruz by Crisógono de Jesús was published in the United States in a translation by Kathleen Pond. In the Foreword, Pond recognizes Peers as the first to make available to the English reader the scholarly work of Saint John of the Cross.

99 Edgar Allison Peers, *Spanish Mysticism: A Preliminary Survey* (London: Methuen, 1924), 3.

100 Peers, 5.

101 It is important to notice that in later studies, such as his short article "Contemporary Spain, Legend and Reality," Peers shows a different perspective on the social history of Spain.

and stands with them in the efforts to reaffirm the greatness of Christianity in Spain – therefore opposing the British discourse of the "dark" Spanish ages. On the other hand, however, a careful reader can perceive in Peers's writings a certain hesitancy to clearly express his opinion about the racial component of Spanish identity pre-sixteenth century. Still, with all its contradictions, Peers's scholarship influenced much of the ways in which academics outside Spain saw Spanish mystical literature.

2.3.1 Edgar Allison Peers vs. Otis Green

I will next revisit one of the most ardent debates about Spanish mystical literature in which Edgar Allison Peers was involved, that with the American scholar Otis H. Green, which took place within the pages of the journal *Hispanic Review*.[102] In his 1939 article "Notes on the Historical Problem of Castilian Mysticism," Otis Green reviews the different arguments about the origin – which he deems a "historical problem" – of Spanish mysticism and contests Peers's argument for the innate mysticism of the Spanish people. Green starts his article by noticing that the period of foundation, growing, flourishing, and decaying of Spanish mysticism can be historically located between the beginning of the sixteenth and the middle of the seventeenth centuries. The time of prosperity in the sixteenth century, Green affirms, was caused by a combination of three elements: the specific historical conditions during the reign of Phillip II (1556–1598); the Counter-Reformation of the Catholic Church as a response to the movement of Reformation in England and the European Low Countries; and what he calls the quality of "genius" of the mystics: "It is thus a manifestation of the national genius which appears when the time is ripe, grows to maturity, and vanishes when the time is over-ripe."[103] He then proceeds to divide the scholarly ideas about the sources of Spanish mystical literature into three, the first being the opinion that Spanish mysticism was "a German import" and that Spanish mystics were influenced by North-German mystics. This thesis is supported, Green notes, by Spanish scholars such as Marcelino Menéndez Pelayo in his books *Historia de las ideas estéticas* and *Historia de los heterodoxos españoles*, and Rafael Altamira in *Psicología del pueblo español*.[104] Akin to Peers, Green rejects this view on the basis that the "Spanish mystics utilized the religious literature that was available to them, whether ancient or

---

102   The journal *Hispanic Review* was the first outside of Spain devoted to Spanish literature and has been continuously published since 1933 by the University of Pennsylvania Press.
103   Otis H. Green, "Notes on the Historical Problem of Castilian Mysticism," *Hispanic Review* 6 (1938), 94.
104   Green, 94–94.

modern, German, Flemish or Italian; not, however, in search of inspiration, but of authority."[105] The second scholarly trend about the origins of Spanish mystical literature that Green identifies is affirming – by mistakenly reading Menéndez Pelayo – that Spanish mysticism owes its rebirth to Renaissance Neoplatonism. Green contends that although Menéndez Pelayo never asserted this, scholars such as Pedro Sáinz Rodríguez make a case for it.[106] For Green, the real influence is not that of Neoplatonism but of the Platonic teaching which could be assimilated by Christian mysticism and which found its way into the works of the Church Fathers, who were widely read by the Spanish mystics. Accordingly, Green affirms that "Neo-Platonism bears to Spanish mysticism the relation not of cause but of effect."[107] The third and final trend that Green finds in the debates about the origins of Spanish mystical literature is that it was "conditioned by causes which were essentially social."[108] To exemplify this third tendency, Green cites Dean William Inge's book *Christian Mysticism*, in which Inge affirms that "the two great Spanish mystics [Santa Teresa, San Juan de la Cruz] were before all things champions of the counter-Reformation."[109] In seeing Spanish mysticism as a reaction to the Reformation, Green seems to be more in agreement with Edgar Allison Peers. Likewise, Green's final conclusion, which does not quite adhere to either of the perspectives that he presents throughout his extensive article, oddly echoes the position of Peers, whom he had set out to refute. For Green, the Spanish mystics are "a literary generation" created by "the leadership of genius":

> That theology became, in sixteenth century Spain, the "ciencia official de una nación en su apogee, que había hecho del catolicismo su bandera colectiva," ["the official science of a nation in its apogee, which had made of Catholicism its collective banner"] may well be ascribed to historical and social causes. That mystical theology came to occupy the great place it did within this general movement is due, in my opinion, to the influence of a few outstanding personalities whose genius was able to impress itself upon the age. We have here all of the elements necessary for the formation of a "literary generation," a group of contemporaries formed by the same intellectual and emotional influences, having abundant contact with each other, faced by a common set of outward circumstances – the

---

105   Green, 97.
106   Green refers specifically to the article "El problema histórico del misticismo español," by Pedro Sáinz Rodriguez (1927).
107   Green, 99.
108   Green, 99.
109   Green, 100.

militant religious spirit of their country and the danger to it from foreign enemies – and inspired by that decisive element which Julius Petersen calls *Führertum* – leadership of genius.[110]

While Green's notion of the "leadership of genius" can be seen as an assumption as subjective as the "innate mysticism" of Peers which fails to provide a satisfactory answer to the "historical problem of Castilian mysticism" that he sought to clarify, his article is key to understanding the dynamics of internal and external orientalism with regard to mystical literature in Spain. The question of Spanish mysticism is as "historical" – as announced in Green's title – as it is political. Asking from where Spanish mystics drew their sources is asking if Spanish mystics were or were not exclusively Christian or if they were influenced by non-Christian and therefore heretical sources, such as Muslims and Jews who lived in Spain – before Spain was Spain – and whose literary production was threatened with erasure from the "history" of Spanish letters notwithstanding the efforts of the Empire and the Inquisition. Moreover, his article and the consequent debate with Peers makes evident the dynamics of external orientalism in the scholarship on Spanish mystical literature. Peers, from England, Green, from the United States, and the other European and North American scholars whom Green cites in his article such as Aubrey F. G. Bell and Ludwig Pfandl, were invested in finding, from outside Spain, the sources of Spanish mystical literature.

In his delayed response to Green, "Notes on the Historical Problem of Castilian Mysticism" (1942), Edgar Allison Peers corrects every other idea proposed by the American scholar, although he acknowledges that Green's argument "lays due stress upon the personal and individual nature of the mystical experience."[111] Peers admits to agreeing in general terms with Green's

---

110 Green, 102–103. Green includes two footnotes in this fragment. The first clarifies that the phrase "the official science of a nation in its apogee, which had made of Catholicism its collective banner" is taken from the article "El problema histórico del misticismo español," by Pedro Sáinz Rodríguez (333–34). The second is a citation for the phrase "leadership of genius," attributed to Julius Petersen, "Die literarischen Generationen," in *Philosophie der literaturwissenschaft*, edited by Emil Ermatinger (Berlin: Junker & Dünnhaupt, 1930), pp. 130–87.

111 Peers, "Notes on the Historical Problem of Castilian Mysticism," *Hispanic Review* 10.1 (1942), 29. Peers affirms that the Spanish scholars – whom Green cites as defenders of the thesis that sixteenth-century Spanish mystical writers were influenced by German mystics – were not well-enough informed about their own tradition. He instead supports the position of the Belgian scholar Pierre Groult, who asserted that the German mystics had some impact but were not imported directly into Spanish soil. Secondly, Peers denies the Platonic and Neoplatonic influence as the cause of the flowering of mysticism in the

argument about the "genius" of the mystics but refutes the socio-historical perspective to insist that in sixteenth-century Spain there was a sudden "mystical eruption."[112] What seems more pressing for Peers in his response is how to frame his certainty that the Spanish are intrinsically mystical. A close examination of Peers's argument shows how it reverts against itself. While he was trying to reaffirm the innate mystical condition of Spain, and with it its Catholicism, Peers was at the same time practicing a mode of external orientalism not by pointing at the oriental features of Spain but by making it an exception.

Peers maintains, as a "view of the truth of which I have long been completely convinced,"[113] that the Spanish are "mystically-minded people" and that this is essential to "the Spanish character."[114] To further sustain this claim, Peers cites the work of scholars – other than those cited by Green – such as the Spanish novelist Andrés Gonzáles-Blanco, who wrote: "We have been mystics in our entrails.... Certainly we have had mysticism inoculated in our race." To this, Peers adds the general judgement of "other foreigners who visit Spain, whether or not they be men of letters" who have commented upon "the traits and incidents which illustrate the mystical element in the Spanish character":[115]

> They observe in the Spaniard's attitude to life a fervent and intense idealism, which, while fully recognizing life's realities (for on these Spaniards always retain a firm hold), is forever impelling him to aim at the object of his desire, and to allow no considerations, whether material or spiritual, to deflect him from his purpose. The Spaniard loathes compromise, and, if his strong sense of reality tells him that he will be ruined unless he abandons his ideals, he will quietly resign himself to accepting ruin.[116]

These observations gathered – as Peers puts it – by foreigners who visit Spain are enough for him to confirm the "character" of the Spanish people and their essential mysticism. Furthermore, Peers adds: "One has only to spend an hour in such a church, early on any morning, to grasp one of the first principles of the mystical life."[117] Whether or not some Spaniards practice religion, they are,

---

sixteenth century, reasoning that Platonic writings were "long before the Renaissance;" and that although Neoplatonism was present in the literature of the period, it cannot be considered as a cause.
112   Peers, "Notes," 29.
113   Peers, "Notes," 18.
114   Peers, "Notes," 18.
115   Peers, "Notes," 20.
116   Peers, "Notes," 20.
117   Peers, "Notes," 21.

according to Peers, all "permeated with the recollectedness, the tranquillity, the singleness of purpose and the passionate devotion of the mystic."[118]

Needless to say, according to today's scholarly standards, affirmations like the ones Peers made would be labeled as extremely subjective and patronizing. Within his own terms, though, Peers's opinion was not negative. He was indeed praising Spain and the Spaniards for their innate religiosity. The fact remains, however, that he was writing from his position as a professor at Liverpool University, summarizing the "Spanish character" with subjective and generalizing terms to affirm that Spaniards are "mystical." Peers's awe of the Spaniards' innate mysticism, and of Spain as a safe haven from the multitudinous religious denominations of Great Britain and the United States, embodies what Howarth calls the "morbid" interests of the English in Spanish religiosity. For Peers, Spain is endlessly mystical in a way that he does not quite explain, ignorant of itself and in need of others to explain its mystical national identity to the rest of the world and to the Spaniards themselves. Thus, his portrait of Spain as a mystical panacea, as the image of the church in the early-morning hours evokes, has a secondary orientalist effect. The same terminology that Peers uses to praise the mystical character of the Spanish people makes evident his orientalist attitude toward Spain. The "oriental" is singled out, made an exception, displaced from the common European trend in the same way that the "mystical" is in Peers's writings. Thus while he was trying to praise Spain for its innate mystical and Christian character, Peers also orientalized it.

Like all other forms of orientalism, Peers's is politically problematic. The austere and religiously committed imagery he represented contradicted the convulsive historical situation that Spain was experiencing in 1942, the year that his response to Green was published. While many Spanish intellectuals were living in exile because of their persecution by the Franco regime, Peers argues not just for Spain's eternal mysticism, but also for Iberia's exclusive Catholic – which in this context meant Francoist – identity. For the British scholar, Spaniards were inherently mystics inasmuch as they also were "the men who waited eight centuries to storm Granada or who poured out their blood to bring peoples in the East or in the West into what they believed to be the one true fold."[119] Furthermore, Peers assessed the social context created by the Francoist government as the perfect space for a "fresh revival of the latent mysticism ... for a new outburst of mystical desire."[120] Peers did not see the

---

118 Peers, "Notes," 21.
119 Peers, "Notes," 21.
120 Peers, "Notes," 32–33.

need to make explicit his political adherences, nor to sort out his arguments' inner contradictions. And neither should we try to do so. But it is relevant to examine such contradictions as a sign of that time, and as an example of the external orientalism that the rest of Europe – and the rest of the Western world – practiced with regard to Spain and its mystical literature.

3   The Scholarship on Spanish Mystical Literature: 1942 and the Next Two Decades

3.1   *Dámaso Alonso and the "Italian Thesis"*

The year that Peers published his response to Green, 1942, marks the celebration of the 500th anniversary of the birth of Saint John of the Cross. This anniversary, as already explained, was extensively manipulated by the National-Catholic regime to reinforce its religious-political agenda. As part of the commemorations, there was a series of scholarly publications that shared what Valente has called "limiting and threatening determinants of fear" which were correlated to Spain's historical circumstances.[121]

The tension between internal and the external orientalism in the scholarship addressing the question of the influences of Spanish mystical writers attained its peak in 1942. In that year, the Spanish writer and scholar Dámaso Alonso published *La poesía de San Juan de la Cruz (desde esta ladera)* (*The Poetry of San Juan de la Cruz (From this Side of the Hill)*). The subtitle of this book, *From this Side of the Hill*, would become a canonical phrase in Spanish literary scholarship given its connotations of what remains "on this side" and "on the other side" of the hill that Alonso evokes. As a framework for this work, Alonso establishes a dialectical separation between the theological or religious and the non-theological and non-religious in analyzing Saint John of the Cross's writings. While he doesn't aim at "excluding the wonder," Alonso announces that he will not deal with such "wonder" as long as there is a human explanation.[122] Taking this dialectical separation between divine and human as his method of inquiry, Alonso follows a literary analysis to prove his "Italian thesis," which advances the idea that the writings of Saint John of the Cross were strongly influenced by Italian poets. Alonso overtly relies on Saint John

---

121   Besides the book by Dámaso Alonso referred in this section, other publications around this date included the *Antología de la poesía sacra española* (*Anthology of Spanish Sacred Poetry*) (1940), edited by José Ángel Valbuena; and Crisógono de Jesus's biography of Saint John of the Cross *Vida de San Juan de la Cruz* (1941), which received the award for the best biography produced during the fourth-centenary celebrations.

122   Alonso, *La poesía de San Juan de la Cruz*, 73.

of the Cross's one-time reference to one verse of the sixteenth-century poet Juan Boscán. From this, he deduces that the mystic was indirectly influenced not just by Boscán but also by Garcilaso de la Vega via the "divinized" poetic versions of Sebastián de Córdoba – who adapted Garcilaso's and Boscán's imagery to the Christian context through the poetic technique that came to be known as *a lo divino*, "divinized," where imagery of non-religious poetry is incorporated into poems with religious motifs.[123] In the endnotes of the second edition of his book, addressing Edgar Allison Peers, Alonso claims that while Saint John of the Cross may not have read Garcilaso and Boscán directly, he was "without any doubt" familiar with the "divinized" poetry of Sebastián de Córdoba. There is no doubt, Alonso affirms, that the Spanish mystic "had in his hands the book of Córdoba and imitated a verse from Cordoba's poem."[124] According to this assumption, he suggests that the influence of Boscán and Garcilaso on the Spanish mystic, although mediated by the divinized versions of Córdoba, is indisputable. But not only does Alonso affirm that Saint John of the Cross was influenced by Boscán and Garcilaso, his "Italian thesis" attributes to the mystic's writings the influence of Italian poets such as Petrarch, whose work had influenced Garcilaso. Accordingly, Alonso concludes that the actual sources of the poetic style of Saint John of the Cross have to be traced back to the Italian Renaissance.

3.1.1 The Alonso–Peers Debate

Not surprisingly, Alonso's "Italian thesis" was strongly opposed by the British scholar Edgar Allison Peers, who published a two-part article arguing against Alonso's thesis.[125] In his response, Peers offers an exhaustive philological critique of every one of the passages by Garcilaso, Boscán, Córdoba, and Saint John of the Cross that Alonso analyzed in his 1942 book. In addition, Peers reviews the previous arguments of the Spanish priest and scholar Crisógono de Jesús (1912–14) and of José Ángel Valbuena (1940), who, like Alonso, defended the thesis of the influence of the poetry of Boscán and Garcilaso via the

---

123 Juan Boscán and Garcilaso de la Vega are two of the most relevant Spanish poets of the sixteenth century, heavily influenced by Italian Petrarchism. In 1575, the poet Sebastián de Córdoba, imitating the style of the Italian Gerolamo Malipiero, published a "divinized" (*a lo divino*) adaptation of Boscán and Garcilaso's poetry, in which the profane love was reinterpreted as love for the divine. This is, according to Alonso and others, the work that influenced Saint John of the Cross.
124 Alonso, *La poesía*, 329.
125 "The Alleged Debt of San Juan de la Cruz to Boscán and Garcilaso de la Vega" (1953), and "The Alleged Debts of San Juan de la Cruz to Boscán and Garcilaso de la Vega (Concluded)" (1953).

divinized versions of Sebastián de Córdoba on Saint John of the Cross's poetic style. Peers concludes that although the resonances of Boscán and Garcilaso's poetry in Saint John of the Cross's cannot be disregarded, "the reminiscences might quite well be the results of impressions formed by reading [Boscán and Garcilaso] in boyhood and never lost, nor need we for any reason suppose more than this unless we so desire."[126] Although Peers does not attempt to elucidate why these Spanish scholars may "desire" to prove an Italian and Romanized influence in the poetry of the Spanish mystic, he does suggest that Alonso and the other followers of the "Italian thesis" have "tended to assume too much," and that the claimed influence should be more accurately understood as a case of reminiscence on topics and figures very familiar to the Spanish lyric with which the mystic could have been familiar.[127] In the endnotes to the second edition of his book (1946), Alonso addresses Peers plainly: "What other choice do we have but to think that these verses come from the divinized Garcilaso?"[128] Relying again on Saint John of the Cross's one-time reference to a verse by Boscán in his commentaries to the *Spiritual Canticle*, Alonso affirms that the mystic "had in his hands the book of Córdoba and imitated a verse from Cordoba's poem."[129]

The Alonso–Peers debate offers a different perspective from the Peers–Green debate that had taken place a decade before. If in the earlier instance we notice two modes of external orientalism, the Alonso–Peers controversy exemplifies the internal-external orientalist tension. In the former case, Peers did not disagree strongly with Green about the idea of the "Spanish genius" but insisted on his perspective of the innate mysticism of the Spanish people. In the later, the English scholar adamantly disagrees with the theories of influence proposed by the Spaniard. Peers's view, with his external orientalism, contrasts with Alonso's effort to prove the exclusive affiliations of Saint John of the Cross with Christian and Latin sources, while both demonstrate an active orientalism.

Alonso's efforts to prove the exclusive affiliations of Saint John of the Cross with Latin sources seem in tune with the historical National Catholic project, which proclaimed the exclusively Roman origins of Spanish culture. As we will discuss later, Spanish critic and writer José Ángel Valente considered that

---

126 Peers, "The Alleged Debt of San Juan de la Cruz to Boscán and Garcilaso de la Vega," 5.
127 Peers, 54. For Peers, the only exception in the scholarship on Spanish mystical literature is the Frenchman Jean Baruzi (1924), whom he describes as a cautious and true scholar who does not rush to make assumptions. It is interesting to notice that, like Peers, Baruzi was not a Spanish scholar.
128 Alonso, *La poesía*, 329.
129 Alonso, *La poesía*, 329.

Alonso's attempt to produce an exclusive philological reading of Saint John of the Cross in order to substantiate his European and Catholic influence is "mutilated beforehand" and is located within the same coordinates of "religious terror" as the reading of Menéndez Pelayo analyzed earlier.[130] Moreover, Alonso's claim to be reading Saint John of the Cross's work "from this side of the hill" became an obstacle to newer and more liberal readings of the work of the mystic, and with it of Spanish mystical writers in general. Nonetheless, Alonso's work is indispensable to a study of the scholarship on Spanish mystical literature because, with all its limits, it became foundational for the field; and because it is a prototype of the internal orientalism that we are examining in the present work.

3.2 Helmut Hatzfeld and the "National Tendencies of Mystical Language"

In 1955, the German philologist and literature scholar Helmut Hatzfeld published in Madrid his *Estudios literarios sobre mística española*, with the same press (Biblioteca Románica Hispánica) that published Dámaso Alonso's 1942 book. Hatzfeld's work presents a particular case in the scholarship on Spanish mysticism as it shares with Alonso's an adherence to the National-Catholic discourse and with Peers's an orientalist tendency in his analysis of Spanish mystical literature. Following a detailed philogenetic analysis of comparison similar to that displayed by Alonso in his *La poesía de San Juan de la Cruz* and later by Peers in his refutation of Alonso's Italian thesis, Hatzfeld sets out to demonstrate the evidence for a historical influence of German mystics, especially of the Fleming Jan Van Ruysbroeck, on the Spanish mystics of the sixteenth century even though he acknowledges that the first Spanish translations of the Flemish were not published until 1593, two years after the death of Saint John of the Cross and eleven after the death of Saint Teresa of Jesus.

While his main argument – the presence of German influences on Spanish mystical writers – differs from that of Alonso, we find in Hatzfeld a nationalist language that echoes that of the Spanish scholar as well as an intention to exclude from his analysis any work written on the Peninsula in a language other than Spanish and at a date prior to 1492.[131] Hatzfeld asserts that the Spanish mystics "used the language, whose grammar had just been fixed by Nebrija, whose rich vocabulary and phrases Covarrubias would reveal, and

---

130   José Ángel Valente, "Introducción," *Hermenéutica y mística*, 10.
131   This, with the sole exception of the Catalan Raymond Llull, whose writings, according to Hatzfeld as well as Peers, carried a "missionary zeal" that justifies his presence in the Spanish imagination and in the work of the mystics of the sixteenth century.

used this language with a creative spirit and for their own purpose."[132] Echoing both Peers and Green, Hatzfeld maintains that the historical conditions of 1492 were propitious for the birth of a "classic, typical and normative mysticism in the eyes of the theologian as well as the student of literature."[133] Such "classic, typical, and normative mysticism" is defined by Hatzfeld in socio-historical terms strictly linked to the so-called *Reconquista*, which implied the expulsion of the Jews and the Muslims from the Iberian Peninsula and the establishment of the Spanish Empire. Hatzfeld writes:

> Just like the *conquistadores* in faraway lands, the mystics from that time pretended to discover new worlds in the interior of their souls by the route of *ensimismarse*.... The souls of the classic ascetics were, like the castles of Castile, raised against the Moors; just that now the castle of the soul (interior castle) is alert and vigilant against the demon instead of against the Moors.[134]

The parallel between "the Moors" and "the demons" is quite apparent in Hatzfeld's language, and so is the link between the castles erected against Muslims and the "interior castles" of Spanish mysticism – referring to Saint Teresa of Jesus's mystical work *The Castles of the Soul*.

Like Dámaso Alonso, Hatzfeld claims European (although not Italian) influences in the poetry of the Spanish mystics; and, like Peers, he defends a particular mystical character of Spanish culture. But his orientalist views – probably influenced by the work of other German philologists and of German Indologists such as Max Muller – are more complicated than the internal orientalism of Alonso and the external of Peers. If, on one hand, Hatzfeld stresses the identification of the Muslims with the devil, on the other hand, he advances ideas such as qualifying the mystical practices of Raymond Llull and Saint Teresa of Jesus with what he terms "a Christian yoga."[135] This kind of generalization demonstrates Hatzfeld's implicit view of the blurry boundaries

---

132 Hatzfeld, *Estudios literarios sobre mística Española*, 20. Antonio de Nebrija is the author of the *First Grammar of the Castilian Language*, published in 1492 and dedicated to Queen Isabel of Castile. Sebastián de Covarrubias is the author of the first Spanish dictionary, *Tesoro de la lengua castellana o española*, published in Madrid in 1611.
133 Hatzfeld, *Estudios literarios*, 17.
134 Hatzfeld, *Estudios literarios*, 257. There is no English equivalent for the term *ensimismar*, which literarily means "to go inside oneself."
135 Hatzfeld, *Estudios literarios*, 51. Hatzfeld constructs his argument on the basis of the two mystics' use of the metaphor of the union to symbolize the encounter of the mystic's soul with God. Relying on a semantic predicament – that *yoga* (in Sanskrit, "union") and *unión* (the Spanish word for "union") have the same etymology – he advances that the poetic

between the Orient and Spain; and of Spanish mystical literature as related to the two – Spain and the oriental.

Still, Hatzfeld's most evident contribution to the external orientalist quest was his incursions into a psychological and historical determinism to explain what he deems to be "the national tendencies of mystical language."[136] Hatzfeld builds this argument upon the theories of the German philologist Eugen Lerch, who, following the school of linguistic idealism, analyzed the syntax and vocabulary of Spanish and French languages to conclude that they correspond to the "men of fantasy" and the "men of reason," respectively. Based upon these dual distinctions, Hatzfeld establishes a difference between meditation – the spiritual practice that he attributes to French mystics who are endowed with the national characteristic of reason – and contemplation – practiced by the Spaniards because they possess the national characteristics of unreason and passion.[137] Within this framework (which also echoes William James's ideas) Hatzfeld compares the writings of mystics from both countries, such as Saint Teresa of Jesus and Marie de l'Incarnation, seeking to prove that the mystical literature produced by them differs according to the national characteristics of irrationality or rationality, respectively. For example, Hatzfeld affirms that one of the features of Spanish mystical literature is the abundance of similes of penetration, while the French mystics were not interested in penetration or immersion, but in a "mediatory" experience.[138] Although in his discussion Hatzfeld seems to favor the rationality of the French mystics over the Spaniards' "lack of control," he concludes by stating that the French mystical writers do not attain the same deep meditative states of the Spanish and that they "express directly their experience of mystical union" while the former "prefer to theorize."[139] With this, Hatzfeld seeks to demonstrate that the national characteristics of the Spanish people – irrationality, passion, and fantasy – favor the attainment of higher degrees in the mystical practices.

Although viewed through a different lens, Hatzfeld's argument clearly echoes the insistence of Peers on the innate mysticism of the Spanish people. Placing both arguments alongside each other, one observes that the "truth" that Peers says to know by experience – that mysticism is innate in Spaniards – is not far from Hatzfeld's ideas on the national characteristics of mystical language. Both scholars, the Briton in 1924 and the German in 1955, advance a

---

images of Llull and Teresa of Jesus are founded on a spiritual practice of what he calls "a Christian yoga" – a notion that he does not define beyond the etymological assumptions.
136 Hatzfeld, *Estudios literarios*, 146.
137 Hatzfeld, *Estudios literarios*, 148.
138 Hatzfeld, *Estudios literarios*, 183.
139 Hatzfeld, *Estudios literarios*, 201.

case for a Spanish distinctiveness which propels the flourishing of mysticism in the sixteenth century. They both construct their arguments upon their own notions of what mysticism is and what Spain is. The "lack of control" and the "excessive passion" that Hatzfeld finds in the Spanish character come to resonate with Peers's image of a church in the early morning hours – for him a symbol of the essence of Spanish mysticism. Peers and Hatzfeld, each within his own intellectual context, define Spain in terms different from the rest of the European continent. Their scholarship also makes evident how the rearranging of the European continent which took place after World War II determined what other European nations Spain would be compared with. If, in 1924, one could talk about an English invention of Spain – as in the case of Peers's theories of an endless, mystical land – during the post-war years, the objects of comparison were Germany and France. In both cases, scholars were placing Spain within the constraints of an orientalist outlook, not only by saying that Spain is different from the rest of Europe (England and France respectively) but also by the ways in which this difference is depicted: being irrational and passionate, as Orientals are meant to be from the European eye.

3.3   Ángel Cilveti and the "Patrimony of Spanish Culture"

A notable switch in Spanish scholarship on the topic of mysticism is to be found in Ángel Cilveti's book *Introducción a la mística española*, published in 1974 – a year before the death of the dictator Francisco Franco and the beginning of democracy in Spain. Cilveti's goal is to offer the reader a clear and systematic description of the different mystical traditions that existed in the Iberian Peninsula. His method unfolds in an effort to balance the value of all religious systems while claiming the superiority of Christianity. Still, this is the first instance of a scholarly work that includes – even if with many caveats – non-Christian and pre-1492 writers as part of what Cilveti calls the "patrimony of Spanish culture," and of Spanish mystical literature. In the Prologue to his book, Cilveti writes:

> Our concept of Spanish mysticism includes not only Christian mysticism but also the Arabic and the Jewish. The inclusion of these is justified, in the first place, for a cultural reason: the mysticism of Ibn 'Arabi and of the Jewish Abulafia has as much right to appear in the Spanish cultural patrimony as does the philosophy of Averroes and Maimonides, which are already included in it. Still, because of their language and ideology, the mysticism and philosophy of these authors is not as essential to the Spanish culture as are the mysticism of Santa Teresa [of Jesus] and the

philosophy of [Francisco] Suárez. This is the reason why we attribute more importance to Christian mysticism than to the Arabic and Jewish.[140]

With these introductory words, Cilveti is calling attention not just to the inclusion of Jewish and Muslim presence in Spanish culture but also to the unequal parameters with which the two have been measured – where the Jewish presence, although Jews were the first ones expelled in 1492, is less conflictive with twentieth-century politics than the Muslim. While claiming that Catholicism and Spanish are the religion and the language "essential" to Spanish culture, Cilveti also argues – for the first time in the scholarship researched for this volume – that Jewish and Muslim mystics are relevant to Spanish literature because they helped to model what he calls the "heroic man" of Iberian mysticism:

> In their mature period, the Arab, Jewish, and Christian Spanish cultures have produced a type of heroic man, the mystic, who extends his conquest to the spheres of the spirit. The works of the Spanish mystics are the culmination of Arabic, Jewish and Christian mysticism and the triumph of the spirit.[141]

In spite of Cilveti's attributing superiority to Christian mystics, and in spite of his defending Hatzfeld's thesis that Spanish mystics were directly influenced by fourteenth-century German and Flemish mystics, his inclusive gesture represents a radical change in the scholarship on Spanish mysticism.

Cilveti's partial but first opening to a broader context for Spanish mystical literature is evident as well in his critique of the Perennialist scholars William James and Evelyn Underhill, whose work we examined at the beginning of this volume. In the first chapter of *Introducción a la mística española*, Cilveti undertakes a detailed description of the mystical experience and argues that the predicament of the school of *Philosophia Perennia* – that the same divine principle is behind every religious experience – is misleading because each mystic describes a divinity "taken from his particular religious creed."[142] Cilveti does not allege a complete identity of the different traditions, as the Perennial philosophers do, but rather a resemblance (*semejanza*) of the mystical phenomenon justified on the concept of experience: "the common idea that

---

140   Ángel L. Cilveti, *Introducción a la mística española*, 9.
141   Cilveti, 10.
142   Cilveti, *Introducción*, 15.

unifies the different traditions is the following paradox: that all is one, in the sense that the one (God, the Beloved, Kali) is apprehended in the multiplicity of things."[143] Cilveti's arguments, founded on the dialectic notion of experience, pose a challenge to the nationalist discourse and to the orientalist undertones of previous scholars who echoed the Perennialists' assumptions.

Cilveti's scholarship, moreover, models what could become a comparative methodology by establishing theological themes – in particular the topic of union – from which to look at mystics from the Christian, Jewish, and Muslim traditions, and sometimes including references to Hinduism. This methodological framework is based upon his scientific outlook of literary analysis: "the student of mysticism pretends not to remove the veil of the ineffable. His role is limited to investigating the second-hand experience that the mystic's declarations provide; that is, the concepts, images, inferences and hypotheses that the mystic uses."[144] Such concepts and images, Cilveti argues further, provide the research material of the scholar. While the ineffability of the experience cannot be understood, it is possible to examine "how mystical language functions."[145] Through an examination of theological concepts and literary imagery, Cilveti finds a "common idea that unifies the different traditions." But he insists that given this unifying commonality, each mystic should be understood within the terms of his or her own tradition.[146]

Cilveti's openness to the particularities of other traditions, however, could appear limited to twenty-first century scholars. Based on what he understands to be "the essence" of the Christian, Jewish, and Muslim traditions, Cilveti claims the superiority of Christianity, given its theistic quality. Regarding this, he could have been echoing the work of R. C. Zaehner, who suggested that different textual descriptions imply different experiences and that, ultimately, the theistic experience is superior to the pantheistic or non-theistic.[147] Just like Zaehner's – and before him Evelyn Underhill's – Cilveti's comparative methodology favors the Christian experience. Notwithstanding the criticism that we can make today of Cilveti's scholarship and his political and theological biases, his 1974 work deserves attention for its groundbreaking statements, methodological coherence, and the structured method he develops. His *Introducción a*

---

143   Cilveti, *Introducción*, 16.
144   Cilveti, *Introducción*, 35.
145   Cilveti, *Introducción*, 52.
146   This approach seems in dialogue with the German scholar Gershom Scholem, who in his *Major Trends in Jewish Mysticism* (1941) – quoted by Cilveti in his footnotes – maintains that the mystic must speak the language of the tradition in order to be understood at all.
147   Robert Charles Zaehner, *Mysticism Sacred and Profane: An Inquiry into Some Varieties of Praeternatural Experience* (Oxford: Clarendon, 1957).

la mística española is a breakthrough in the internal/external orientalist scholarly dynamics on the topic of Spanish mystical literature.

4 The Scholarship on Spanish Mystical Literature: The Turn of the Century

4.1 Luce López-Baralt: From "Where?" to "What?"

Fifty years passed with no explicit dialogue with the comparative enterprise of Miguel Asín Palacios until his findings were re-examined by Luce López-Baralt, who declares herself a disciple of Asín Palacios in her first book, *San Juan de la Cruz y el Islam* (1985).[148] But the work of this prolific scholar is much more than a continuation of Asín Palacios's ideas. López-Baralt's scholarship draws the trajectory from the historical question of origins – Asín Palacios's question of "Where" to find the hidden connection between the Spanish Christian and the Sufi poets – to the question of "What" there is to learn from Spanish mystical literature alongside mystics from other traditions even when there is no historical connection. This transition from "Where?" to "What?", evident in López-Baralt's work, demonstrates a scholarly coherence and a methodological flexibility that redefined the scholarship on Spanish mystical literature at the end of the twentieth century and into the beginning of the new millennium. In María Rosa Menocal's words, Luce López-Baralt "skillfully constructs a literary history that eventually excludes most traditional Graeco-Roman sources as the possible heritage for San Juan's radical new techniques."[149] No less relevant is the fact that López-Baralt is the first woman and the first Latin American scholar to seriously commit to a comparative approach to Spanish mystical literature. Although she started her career in the United States and continued it in her native Puerto Rico, *San Juan de la Cruz y el Islam* was published in Mexico because no Spanish publisher would take the risk of "unburying" Asín Palacios's controversial ideas. In writing and publishing from the Americas, López-Baralt also changed the dynamics that until then had practically dominated the sholarship on Spanish mystical literature. Moreover, her

---

148 López-Baralt's first book has a very similar title to the English translation of Asín Palacios's article, "Un precursor hispanomusulmán de San Juan de la Cruz," translated by Howard W. Yoder and Elmer H. Douglas as *Saint John of the Cross and Islam*, Vantage Press, New York, 1981. The original article appeared in the journal *Al-Andalus*, vol. 1 (1933), 7–79; then in *Huellas del Islam*, Espasa-Calpe (Madrid, 1941), 235–304; and also in the *Obras escogidas*, vol. 1 (Madrid, 1946), 243–326.

149 María Rosa Menocal, review of *Don Miguel Asín Palacios: Mística cristiana y mística musulmana*, by José Valdivia Valor, *Hispanic Review* 64 no. 2 (1996): 378.

work promoted what we may call a new school of comparativists who, from the other side of the Atlantic, are now producing innovative scholarship on Spanish mystical literature.

Although López-Baralt sees herself as the intellectual heir of the controversial Miguel Asín Palacios, her work radically changed her predecessor's argument and, eventually, his methodology. In *San Juan de la Cruz y el Islam*, López-Baralt affirms that the literary and theological similarities between Sufi and Christian mystics indicates not a Christianized Islam – as Asín Palacios had argued – but an Islamized Christianity, which she deems tangible in the poetic parallelisms of Saint John of the Cross's writings with Iberian and non-Iberian Sufi poetry. Examining Asín Palacios's assumptions, López-Baralt finds that, in fact, the Muslim mystics had borrowed certain "rudiments" from primitive Christians and they had, over the centuries, incorporated those borrowings into their tradition. However, by the time Sufism flowered in Al-Andalus (the southern part of today's Spain), those early borrowings from Oriental Christianity displayed intricate features that were organically Islamic, not Christian Neoplatonic as Asín Palacios had thought. Such uniquely Muslim symbols, according to López-Baralt, are precisely what readers find in the writings of Saint John of the Cross.

With this critical amendment to Asín Palacios's foundational thesis, López-Baralt's early scholarship reiterates his historical question: "Where to find" that historical moment of encounter between Saint John of the Cross and the Sufi tradition? Echoing her predecessor's statements, she writes that the literary evidence for a familiarity of Saint John of the Cross with Sufi poets such as Ibn 'Arabi and Ibn 'Alfarid was a "fascinating enigma and an authentic historical-literary problem,"[150] as well as "too much specificity to be a casual coincidence."[151] López-Baralt locates the literary evidence for such familiarity in features of Saint John of the Cross's writing which cannot be traced within the European context and had seriously challenged early scholars such as Marcelino Menéndez Pelayo and Dámaso Alonso. Accordingly, in *San Juan de la Cruz y el Islam*, she examines in detail a series of parallelisms between the Spanish mystic and the Sufi writers, such as the attribution of more than one meaning to the same word, the absence of verbs in parallel descriptive expressions, and the specific use of poetic images like the fountain and the solitary bird, all of which Saint John of the Cross adopts in a fashion long cultivated

---

150   Luce López-Baralt, *San Juan de la Cruz y el Islam* (México, D.F.: Colegio de México, Centro de Estudios Lingüísticos y Literarios, 1985), 229.
151   López-Baralt, 230.

among the Sufis and unprecedented in European traditions. One of the more striking conclusions at which she arrives in her first book is that these qualities of Saint John of the Cross's writings appear to be rarely familiar with the hermetic principles of the *Trobar Clus* – a coded Sufi poetical style which, in its beginnings, was accessible only to initiated Sufi writers and later became a standardized literary convention, although only inside the Islamic tradition.[152] Considering such evidence, López-Baralt strives to support the hypothesis of historical contact initiated by Asín Palacios. However, at the end of her study, she frankly acknowledges that there is a lack of historical proof to support this hypothesis and leaves the historical question open to further research.

López-Baralt's courageous act of reinstating Asín Palacios's historical quest, and then recognizing that history did not easily validate her (and his) thesis, has broad implications for the orientalist scholarly tendencies that we have been examining in this study. How would Spanish literary history change if scholars could demonstrate that Saint John of the Cross had indeed read Arabic and knew the cryptic system of Sufi sects, as López-Baralt suggests? And what would change, religiously, if we were to discover that this Spanish Doctor of the Roman Catholic Church was hiding Sufi codes in his writings? Or if he, despite being a sincere Catholic, had been so familiar with Sufism as to be liable for condemnation by the Inquisition and never to be read or heard about, as happened with many *moriscos* in the sixteenth century on the eve of their final expulsion in 1609? These are – although not clearly articulated – the inquiries at work in López-Baralt's insistence in the "too many evidences" of literary similitude. Nonetheless, this scholar seems to have become aware that the historical question of "Where?" undermined the scope of her research topic: the dialogue between Spanish mystical literature and mystics' works from other religious traditions. If a "where" frames a comparative project, then its absence, the verification of a "nowhere," will mean the end of the comparative enterprise.

At this methodological crossroads, López-Baralt creatively opts for continuing examining both paths. First, with a renewed methodological approach, she moves from the historical question of "Where?" to the comparative question of "What?" In her book *Asedios a lo indecible: San Juan de la Cruz canta al éxtasis transformante* (1998), she asks not for the historical contact between Saint John of the Cross and the Sufi Trobar Clus but what is to be learned from the comparison of Saint John of the Cross's writing and Sufi poets even without the possibility of a direct influence:

---

152   López-Baralt, 229.

> [T]he mystical texts of San Juan and his Muslim predecessors dialogue with each other and are enormously enriched when facing each other, even without considering the possibility of a literary influence of Sufi spirituality on the work of the Reformer.[153]

With this statement, López-Baralt affirms the validity of a comparison beyond the historical quest. Insightfully and rigorously, she proceeds to examine, in her 1998 work, the linguistic details of Saint John of the Cross's poetry and commentary alongside Sufi poets from within and outside the Iberian tradition. The book's title, *Asedios a lo indecible*, roughly translated as *Sieges to the Unsayable*, announces the author's commitment to examining the qualities of language in mystical texts across traditions. She attains this by focusing on specific poetic imagery to investigate how language functions in the Spanish, Arabic, and Persian languages to convey that which is ultimately unsayable. On the other hand, López-Baralt does not completely abandon Asín Palacios's historical quest, but rather re-contextualizes it. In *A la zaga de tu huella: La enseñanza de las lenguas semíticas en Salamanca en tiempos de san Juan de la Cruz* (2006), she claims to prove, by virtue of archival evidence, the likelihood that the Spanish mystic had taken, or at least had been in contact with, Arabic classes taught at the Universidad de Salamanca while he was a student there.

López-Baralt's work on Saint John of the Cross constitutes the clearest answer given to Menéndez Pelayos's legendary "religious terror" when facing the mystic's oriental poetry. Without renouncing the historical quest inherited from Asín Palacios, her effective methodological turn switches attention from the problem of historical filiations to a comparative project for the sake of enriching the reading of texts. With this, López-Baralt responds, from within the field of Spanish mystical literature, to the interdisciplinary call to concentrate on the particularities of mystical language that was commonly emerging among scholars of religion, theology, and literature toward the end of the twentieth century. López-Baralt's scholarship extended a bridge from the "Where?" to the "What?", from the question of affiliations or transmissions to the question of convergences, all the most relevant to today's scholarship.

4.2 José Ángel Valente: Beyond Transmission and Convergences

A critical review of the scholarship on Spanish mystical literature would not be complete without mention of the work of José Ángel Valente, who, like Luce López-Baralt, represents a revolutionary change in the scholarship on this

---

153 López-Baralt, *Asedios a lo Indecible: San Juan de la Cruz canta al éxtasis transformante* (Madrid: Editorial Trotta, 1998), 17.

topic – particularly within Spain. I will first refer to two of his critical essays: "Sobre el lenguaje de los místicos: convergencia y transmisión" (1991) ("About the language of the mystics: convergence and transmission"); and the chapter "Formas de lectura y dinámica de la tradición" ("Forms of reading and dynamics of the tradition"), which was published in the 1995 volume *Hermenéutica y mística: San Juan de la Cruz* (*Hermeneutics and mysticism: Saint John of the Cross*), edited by José Ángel Valente himself and José Lara Garrido.[154] Together, these two essays exemplify the position of Valente as a critic of Spanish mystical literature concerned about the direction that scholarship had taken from the early twentieth century, including the work of authors discussed here. Secondly, I will call attention to Valente's own readings of Spanish mystical literature. While taking seriously the question of transmission and convergences, with its orientalist implications, Valente proposes and exemplifies a method to move beyond those quests and into the terrain of language, which for him is the terrain of a more open dialogue.

José Ángel Valente begins the essay "Sobre el lenguaje de los místicos: convergencia y transmisión" by citing the American scholar Rudolf Otto, who, in his book *Mysticism East and West* (1932) suggests that one can find "homogeneous structures in the mystical phenomena, whatever their latitude and time may be."[155] Supporting Otto's views, Valente points out that without excluding the many distinctions between traditions, the focus on such "homogenous structures" allows for an exploration of mystical literature that moves beyond the quest for direct transmission and into a dialogue that is not preconditioned by historical traces. Accordingly, Valente continues, the comparativist of mystical literatures should carefully separate "the phenomena of convergence from the phenomena of transmission. In fact, the analogical path continues to produce surprising results."[156] While this declaration seems to be hinting at the "comparison by analogy" proposed by Miguel Asín Palacios in his *Christianized Islam*, it deploys a completely different methodology. For Valente, it is indispensable to not just separate the question of convergence from the questions of transmission but to place the focus of analysis beyond both convergence and transmission and into the terrain of language.

Valente's proposal to separate the inquiry into the historical transmission of mystical texts from the examination of their linguistic and poetic convergences

---

154 José Ángel Garrido is a professor of Spanish literature at the Universidad de Málaga, Spain. His research focuses on literature of Al-Andalus, sixteenth-century poetry, and the Spanish literary canon.
155 Rudolf Otto, *Mysticism East and West*, 371.
156 José Ángel Valente, "Sobre el lenguaje de los místicos: convergencia y transmisión," 372.

in the scholarship on Spanish mystical literature does not do away, however, with the critical question of the oriental influences on Western mysticism in general, and particularly on Spanish mystical literature. He addresses this topic by acknowledging that Western Mysticism has "the oriental as the root," and that there is a "natural orientalism" in Western Christian mystical writings.[157] Expressions such as "the oriental as the root" (*La orientalidad como raíz*) and "natural orientalism" (*la natural orientalidad*) refer, in general resonance with Asín Palacios's thesis, to the origins of Christian mysticism, as known in the West, in the context of Christian oriental monasticism: "The more Western mysticism tends toward its most extreme forms, the more it re-encounters its origin and the more it converges toward its natural orientalism."[158] As an example of such "natural orientalism," Valente recalls that Carmelite mysticism had its origins on the Mount of Carmel during the thirteenth century. Like Asín Palacios, Valente highlights the fact that the Carmelite Spanish sixteenth-century tradition is "the most explicitly marked by the idea of contemplative life of the Oriental monasticism."[159]

Valente agrees with Asín Palacios that it would be incoherent to argue for a separation of the East from the origins of Christian mysticism, and thus from Spanish mysticism. Nonetheless, he develops a serious critique of Asín Palacios's argument for a direct transmission, and, thus, a historical relation between Islam and Early Christianity. Valente critiques Asín Palacios's perspective on two fundamental bases: first, that Asín Palacios's thoughts were "obscured" by his religious commitment, which made him insist on the superiority of Christian mysticism to any other kind of mysticism; and secondly, that by focusing on the Muslim tradition, Asín Palacios ignored the overwhelming presence of spiritual traditions inherited from the *conversos* – the Jews who converted to Christianity after 1492 – in Spain during the sixteenth century.[160] As an example of Asín Palacios's failure to look into the correct sources of influence for the Spanish mystics, Valente cites his own argument that the image of the seven castles in Saint Teresa of Jesus's famous book *Las siete moradas* (*The Interior Castle*) has its origin in a Sufi symbol. Instead, Valente argues, Asín

---

157 Valente, 375.
158 Valente, 375.
159 Valente, "Sobre el lenguaje," 375. The original order of the Brothers of Carmel was founded by Saint Albert (Albert Avogadro), who, in imitation of the prophet Elias, became a hermit on the Mount of Carmel, in today's Israel.
160 Valente supports his critique of Miguel Asín Palacios's thesis with the help of the work of the prominent French historian Marcel Bataillon – *Erasme et l'Espagne: Recherches sur l'histoire spirituelle du XVIe siècle* (1937) – who demonstrates the strong presence of *conversos* in Spanish culture after 1492. In this section, Valente also cites the article "Textes musulmans pouvant concerner la nuit de l'espirit," by Louis Massignon.

Palacios should have looked into the Jewish origins of this image in Hekhalot literature, particularly in the school of the Merkabah, which draws many of its symbols from the first chapter of the Book of Ezequiel. In these texts, Valente finds a more credible predecessor of the image of the interior castle with seven rooms developed in the saint's major work. Saint Teresa of Jesus's Jewish ancestors, Valente affirms, would make this kind of influence more credible than that of the Sufi imagery defended by Asín Palacios.

To his critique of Asín Palacios's thesis that there is a direct Sufi influence on the sixteenth-century Spanish mystics Valente adds his account to the early work of Luce López-Baralt, who, as discussed above, reassesses Asín Palacios's ideas. López-Baralt, Valente opines, is far from "solving the problem of filiation" because her proposal is but "a risky simplification" and claims ownership over the essence of a symbol.[161] Nonetheless, in a footnote to his article, Valente admits to be aware of a recent conference presentation where López-Baralt mentioned the possible Jewish influence on Spanish sixteenth-century mysticism by means of the mysticism of the Merkabah school. With this gesture, Valente writes, López-Baralt had partially repaired the limits of Asín Palacios and his fellow scholars of Islam.[162]

A resonant argument against the biases of the scholarly works produced in Spain about mystical literature is found in Valente's contribution to the 1995 collection of essays *Hermenéutica y mística: San Juan de la Cruz* (*Hermeneutics and mysticism: Saint John of the Cross*). This volume, which has yet to receive the attention that it deserves, marks a turning point in the scholarship on Spanish mysticism. Including works from Spanish and non-Spanish scholars, the publication's goal is "breaking through certain hegemonic modes of interpretation ... stagnated academicism ... and canonical schematizations" which originated in a patronizing attitude that determines who writes and what is written about Spanish mysticism.[163] Instead, the editors state in the Prologue, this volume seeks "to abandon discursive codes" that fail to include the aesthetic dimension in their analysis of the work of this important Spanish mystic.[164] Accordingly, their methodological aim is "to repair the relation between mysticism and language," which had been first claimed by Jean Baruzi, but had not been developed further.[165] With this, Valente and Garrido place the scholarship on Saint John of the Cross within the

---

161 Valente, "Sobre el lenguaje," 380.
162 Valente, 380–81.
163 Valente and Garrido, eds., *Hermenéutica y mística*, 9.
164 Valente and Garrido, eds., 11.
165 They are explicitly referring to the book *St. Jean de la Croix et le Problème de l'Expérience Mystique*, published by Jean Baruzi in 1924.

context of "a prioritizing position in the field of human sciences: the reflection about language."[166]

Valente's contribution, the first in the volume, is titled "Formas de lectura y dinámica de la tradición" ("Forms of reading and dynamics of the tradition"). This essay opens with a critique of the ways in which Spanish history has been manipulated and how such manipulations have set strict limits on the scholarship on Spanish mysticism, particularly but not exclusively during the Franco regime.[167] As an instance of such modes of manipulation, Valente recalls the celebration of three prominent Christian anniversaries: the anniversary of the birth of Saint Ignacio of Loyola, founder of the Jesuit Order, celebrated in 1956; the anniversary of the Carmelite Reform, in 1962; and the five-hundredth anniversary of the birth of Saint John of the Cross, in 1942. This last date coincided, as Valente remarks, with "the paroxysm of the triumphal ardor of the Spanish National-Catholicism" (16). All these celebrations, we have noted earlier, were extensively manipulated by the Franco regime in order to reaffirm the ideal of an eternal, Christian Spain.

It is not surprising that Valente first mentions, as an exemplary instance of how the manipulation of Spain's history influenced scholarship on mystical literature, the speech offered by Marcelino Menéndez Pelayo at his induction into the Royal Academy of the Spanish Language, the first work examined in this volume. Menéndez Pelayo's speech, in Valente's opinion, set the tone for the "syndrome of terror" that would guide, or rather misguide, the scholarly work on the Spanish mystic produced in the first half of the twentieth century:

> To declare oneself possessed by terror, to postpone the capacity of judgement, to continue relegating the key of the Spanish poetic tradition in a narrow and separated region: that is the position established until the 1942 centenary with grave consequences.[168]

Such "grave consequences," in Valente's words, brought about a kind of "acritical work," characterized by a "hagiographical triviality" where "only a partial analysis of his [Saint John of the Cross's] poetic work is accomplished by those following the precept of the 'religious terror.'"[169] The historical circumstances of 1942, Valente adds, "seemed to invite – if not to force – a scholarly superficiality that struggled to prevent accusations of 'irreverence' and 'profanation.'"[170]

---

166   Valente and Garrido, eds., *Hermenéutica y mística*, 12.
167   Valente, "Formas de lectura," 15.
168   Valente, 16.
169   Valente, 17.
170   Valente, 16. Here Valente is partially citing from Colin Thompson, who, in his book *The Poet and the Mystic* (1977), criticizes the lack of analysis of John of the Cross's writings

As Valente maintains, the consequences of Pelayo's "syndrome of terror" in the scholarship on Spanish mysticism, affected as they were by the historical circumstances of the first half of the twentieth century in Spain, lasted several decades. Two instances of such a tendency to which he calls attention are the book *La poesía de San Juan de la Cruz: Desde esta ladera*, by Dámaso Alonso; and the essay "Lenguaje insuficiente: San Juan de la Cruz o lo inefable místico" ("Insufficient language: Saint John of the Cross or the Ineffable Mysticism"), published by Jorge Guillén in his book *Lenguaje y Poesía* in 1962.[171] In these works, Valente finds an apparent lack of connection between thought and text (*pensamiento y texto*). Studies like these, in Valente's opinion, reduced and limited the interpretations of the mystics by proclaiming a dualistic separation of the divine and the human, of the spirit and the letter. In the case of Alonso, Valente argues, one finds "a reading mutilated beforehand" that vaguely aims to read Saint John of the Cross's poetry without dealing with its religiosity.[172] In Guillén, on the other hand, Valente notes "a reading inspired by a vulgar dualistic criteria," where the kingdom of the spirit is kept not just far from, but in antagonism with, the human realm.[173] In both, Valente discovers traces of Menéndez Pelayo's "syndrome of terror" and its resulting trivialization and lack of rigor in the study of mystical texts.[174]

4.2.1 José Ángel Valente on the Language of the Mystics
In the two critical articles that we have just commented on, José Ángel Valente argues that scholars need to move beyond the question of influences and into the question of convergences in the language of the Spanish mystics; but he does not offer specific examples of how this should be done. To really understand Valente's methodological commitment to bringing attention to the language of the mystics, it is necessary to look into his own writings about their works. Valente published several essays about mystical literature, focusing specifically on the work of Saint John of the Cross. His critical questions are directed at the subtleties displayed in the details of the poetic language that

---

        among the many scholarly works published in commemoration of the five-hundredth anniversary of his birth.

171   Jorge Guillén, *Lenguaje y poesía: Algunos casos españoles* (Madrid: Revista de Occidente, 1962).
172   Valente, 20.
173   Valente, 21.
174   We should notice, however, that in criticizing Dámaso Alonso for separating the human from the divine, and Jorge Guillén for inviting the reading of John of the Cross's poetry as "merely human," Valente's position, far from defending an exclusivist religious or theological kind of reading, is stepping beyond the dualist perspective in which the human and the divine are regarded apart from each other. What Valente wants is to turn attention to the possibilities of investigating the language of the mystics.

the mystical poet uses: what is the function of language in a mystical text? How does the mystic poet conceive of the act of writing? Valente writes – in a style that is practically untranslatable into English – of how the poetic act and the mystical experience converge within the realm of poetry:

> Paradoxically, the unsayable looks for the act of saying ... the amorphic seeks out form.... The experience of what has no form searches for the act of saying.... The mystic needs to access his own experience by means of poetics.... At the point of maximum tension, when the language is about to explode, great poetry is produced and the unsayable remains infinitely said. It is the infinitude of the act of saying the unsayable that perpetually makes poetry a second language.[175]

For Valente, poetic language is the means by which the mystical experience takes form. Language bridges the experience that takes place beyond the boundaries of time and space with the precise time and space that contextualize the act of writing. Insisting on the capacity of language to communicate some of the mystical experience, Valente moves not only past the dualisms of "human and divine" but also the dualisms of apophasis and cataphasis.[176] Instead, Valente finds that the language of the mystics is neither apophatic nor cataphatic because the non-saying quality of the former is contained and not denied in the saying quality of the latter. Therefore, the question is not whether the language of the mystical texts is saying or unsaying but how the mystic writer uses words to simultaneously say and not say.

Different from other scholars of mystical literature, Valente, who also was a poet, reaffirms the inherent capacity of poetic language to convey the revelation of the mystical experience:

> The revelation of the spirit is only possible in the measure that is locked within the letter and this [the letter] remains in a terrible birthing tension because of what it contains within itself and, at the same time, cannot hold.[177]

As claimed by Valente, the power to maintain such unholdable tension is an intrinsic characteristic of poetic language, and it is not granted by the spiritual

---

175   Valente, "La hermenéutica y la cortedad del decir," 87.
176   According to Dionysius the Areopagite, mystical language expresses divine truths by means of a cataphatic method, from the Greek *kataphaticos*, "affirmative speech," or by an apophatic method, from the Greek *apophatikos*, "denying speech."
177   Valente, "Verbum absconditum," 397.

experience which is being poured into it through the process of mystical writing. In that sense, poetic language lends itself to being the container of the religious experience while remaining independent from it:

> The words of the mystic postulates something impossible.... But such is, and no other, the ultimate and true root of the poetic word ... the impossible, the unsayable which takes the word to its maximum tension.[178]

Having at its core that exact capacity to say the unsayable, poetic language concurs with, and turns into, the language of the mystic:

> That impossibility of abbreviation to one given sense is one of the main convergent points of the language of the poet and the language of the mystic and, likewise, of their respective subjacent experiences.[179]

According to Valente, the experience of the poet and the experience of the mystic share in a sense of irreducibility. The difference is that the poet reaches this experience by intimate labor with language while the mystic does it by an encounter with God. But when the poet is the mystic, as in the case of Saint John of the Cross, the irreducibility of the mystical experience repeats itself in the irreducibility of language.

It is in this tension between language and experience, in this struggle to approach with words that which is irreducible, where Valente finds moments of convergence among mystics from different traditions. Although in his writings he does not develop a comparison *per se*, we can perceive a movement toward comparison anchored in language. For instance, in the short essay "El ojo del agua" ("The eye of water"), Valente examines one of the most provocative stanzas written by Saint John of the Cross through the lens of the Islamic tradition, particularly the writings of Rūmī.[180] His intention, far from that of the scholars he contests, is not to claim a genealogical relation between the Spanish and the Sufi mystics but to expand the context for reading and interpreting Spanish mystical literature. He does not aim to prove that Saint John of the Cross was in any contact whatsoever with Islamic sources but that he belongs to "a mystical tradition ... in which vertebral elements reappear at all times, latitude or religious context in which the experience of the mystic

---

178   Valente, 397.
179   Valente, 405.
180   Rūmī (13th century) is one of the most influential Sufi poets of all times. His poetry, written in Persian and Arabic, has had a great impact on Western mystical literature.

is manifested."[181] Accordingly, the poetic codes of other traditions may lend themselves to reading the poetry of the Spanish mystics, and vice versa, if one is willing to put aside the "anxiety of influence" that dominated early and mid-twentieth-century scholarship on Spanish mysticism.

While Valente's claims may sound obvious to today's scholars, within his era he was breaking through a tradition heavily imposed on scholarship, mostly by politics, to either strictly separate or historically relate Spanish mysticism to "the oriental." For Valente, as he writes in this critical essay, the oriental is to be understood as "the root" of Western mystical tradition, and "oriental" symbols converge with those of the Spanish mystics, without assuming a philogenetic connection between the two. In asserting so, Valente's scholarship marks a turning point. On one hand, he reassesses, and plainly refutes, the position of early scholars such as Miguel Asín Palacios for their limited attention to the real sources of historical convergence and for the ease with which they established a genealogical connection between symbols shared by Sufis and Spanish mystics. On the other hand, he criticizes the work of Dámaso Alonso and Jorge Guillén for a lack of connection "between thought and text." Both of them, Valente insists, inherited a damaging tendency to trivialize mystical literature in order to comply with political predicaments. In his own work, then, he focuses intensely on the interstices of the mystics' poetic language, and it is there, not in the search for historical convergences, where Valente finds an entry point into the dialogue with other mystical traditions.

4.3 *Eulogio Pacho: Relations and Dependencies*

We will now conclude this extended critical surveyed by examining a brief but powerful work by Eulogio Pacho, written toward the end of his life in 2005. Like Asín Palacios, and each within his own time frame, Eulogio Pacho represents a particular kind of dual commitment to scholarship and to a religious identity.[182] As both were Catholic priests and active scholars, their academic approaches converse in particular ways into which I cannot delve here. In addition, Pacho collaborated amply with Luce López-Baralt and wrote the first *Diccionario de San Juan de la Cruz*. From Pacho's copious bibliography, I will focus on the chapter "Simientes neerlandesas de la mística española," published in the collection of essays *Fuentes neerlandesas de la mística española* (2005). This volume revisits the topic of the Northern European influences on the writing of the Spanish mystics, previously explored in the work of scholars such

---

181   Valente, "El ojo del agua," 316.
182   Eulogio Pacho was a Carmelite priest and scholar who devoted his career to investigate the work of the Carmelite mystics, particularly of Saint John of the Cross.

as Helmut Hatzfeld, examined here. Arguing that the Spanish mystics were actually influenced by Northern European mystics was, in the early and mid-twentieth century, a way of bypassing the orientalist influences and of reaffirming the Catholic and European character of Spanish culture. But, in the early twenty-first century, it takes a different approach.

In his opening chapter, Pacho offers a brief but relevant reflection on the methodological premises that a scholar should follow to clearly elucidate the difference between the so-called "relations" and the so called "dependencies" regarding the writings of Spanish mystics and mystics from other traditions. Although Pacho's chapter focuses specifically on the question of influences of Northern European mystics on the work of Spanish sixteenth-century mystics, his methodological criteria can model any approach to a comparison of Spanish mystical literature. His ideas, as we will next observe, resonate with Valente's insistence in the need of separating convergences from influences, and with López-Baralt question of "What?"

Pacho starts by stating that too much has been assumed in the scholarship on mystical texts produced in Spain in the twentieth century. Although he does not mention specific names, as Valente does, he clearly expresses his concern: "Frequently, the contextualization of spiritual topics leads to fictitious or inexact phenomena of dependency because the critic assumes implicitly or explicitly an authorial originality that is not correct."[183] By warning against overly-assumed influences, Pacho is insisting, at the start of the twenty-first century, on the necessity to establish a clear framework for the scholarship of Spanish mystical literature that does away with the political and orientalist agendas of the criticism produced earlier. There are, Pacho states, relationships between mystical texts which should not be understood as dependences. One instance is poetic imagery, such as a series of symbols inherited from the Medieval Patristic tradition – like iron and firewood, a stone and the center, and the ascending fire. When such images appear in the writing of the Spanish mystics, they are to be taken as phenomena of relationships and not as a direct dependence. On the same note, Pacho continues, there are "natural or spontaneous convergences" because "faced with similar or identical spiritual circumstances the human psychology reacts more or less the same way; the same spiritual experiences tend naturally to identical or similar manifestations."[184] These, too, should not be considered examples of direct influence of dependence. A direct influence between mystical texts, Pacho

---

183 Pacho, "Simientes neerlandesas," 21.
184 Pacho, 21. Although this statement could seem an inclination toward Perennialism, it is important to notice that Pacho is not assuming, as the Perennialists did, that the mystical

maintains, should only be hypothesized by a scholar when it is clearly stated in the text in question or when it can be undoubtedly established by the comparative analysis of texts. But that is not the case with most of the arguments of influence made by the scholarship produced in Spain, particularly during the early and mid-twentieth century. As Pacho writes, in the case of doctrinal or linguistic convergences "one can only affirm an actual dependency if there is specific data.... The coincidence on a topic, a word or traditional imagery is not enough."[185]

Following his own methodological premises, Pacho concludes his article by stating that although the presence of Northern European mystics is obvious, particularly in the mid-sixteenth century – given specific Spanish translations that were published and circulated in the peninsula – its direct influence is less than has been assumed. In doing so, he is dismantling the scholarly-political agenda followed by critics such as Hatzfeld. This brief section of Pacho's chapter is a brilliant guideline for any comparative work on Spanish mysticism, and for mystical literature in general.

In López-Baralt, Valente, and Pacho, we find late twentieth-century scholarship on Spanish mystical literature moving progressively beyond orientalist and geopolitical agendas which characterized and, to an extent, hindered the works produced earlier. Focusing on how language operates in mystical texts across different traditions, and doing so not for the sake of proving a historical connection but of deepening the analysis of Spanish mystical literature, these scholars opened the door to conversations across disciplines and traditions.

Conclusions: The Scholarship on Spanish Mystical Literature: Its Present and Future

This critical surveyed has examined the work of twentieth-century scholars on Spanish mystical literature, paying particularly attention to how their notions about Spain's geopolitical position in the world map, particularly in relationship to the Orient, affected their scholarly approaches to this contested topic. We have followed a general chronological structure, observing how their ideas about the works of Spanish mystical writers varied over periods of time according to their notions about Spain's location in the European geopolitical map. The earliest work we analyzed in detail was *Christianized Islam* (1924), by one of the most controversial Spanish scholars of all times, Miguel Asín

---

experience is the same across different religious traditions but that there are similar reactions.

185 Pacho, 22.

Palacios; and the last one was a brief but exemplary summary of the methodology of comparative literature by Eulogio Pacho (2005). The eighty years between Asín Palacios and Pacho were divided into three general periods: first, we examined the scholarship produced prior to 1942. The second period, then, included the scholarship produced in and following 1942, which marked the appearance of several publications within the context of the celebration of the five-hundredth anniversary of Saint John of the Cross's birth. The third period encompassed the works published in the years after the end of the Franco dictatorship in Spain and into the early twenty-first century. For each of these three periods, we have focused on a selected number of scholarly works which exemplify distinct approaches to Spanish mystical literature, including works published both inside and outside Spain, and written by Spanish and other European, North American, and Latin American scholars. This thematic survey demonstrates that the foundational scholarship on Spanish mystical literature which we still read, cite, and teach was conditioned by geopolitical and orientalist biases which should be carefully considered.

Now, before moving to our conclusive thoughts, a word of clarification: I have used the late twentieth-century category of orientalism, and the related concept of geopolitics, to analyze the work of scholars who wrote and thought about Spanish mystical literature in an environment embedded with notions different from those we hold and value today. Moreover, the world map and its politics were drastically changing during the time period covered in this study. We could not have asked Menéndez Pelayo, Asín Palacios, or Edgar Allison Peers – not even Dámaso Alonso or Helmut Hatzfeld – to be aware of their orientalist biases. Even less could we have asked them to be coherent in the eyes of the future with which we look at them. Their ideas, often revolutionary for their own times, received both praise and blame from their contemporaries. This study has not sought in any way to diminish the merit of their scholarly contributions. In fact, I think that their work should be examined and taught more in-depth than it is nowadays. What I would like is for my reader to observe, with a sense of self-awareness, what we can learn from their scholarly practices.

Clearly, the scholarly landscape in Spain has changed much in the almost half a century after the death of Francisco Franco and the establishment of the Spanish democracy. Today, one of the most active scholarly institutions at the center of debates about Spanish mystical literature is the Centro Internacional Teresiano-Sanjuanista (CITeS), also called "Universidad de la Mística" and situated in Ávila.[186] Founded in 1986, the CITeS is a religious and academic

---

186 The name of this institution, practically untranslatable into English, evokes the names of Saint Teresa of Jesus (*Teresiano*) and Saint John of the Cross (*Sanjuanista*). The city of

institution, directed by Discalced Carmelite monks who are also scholars of mystical literature. The goal of the center, its website states, is "to promote the systematic study of the lives and works of these saints and Doctors of the Church [the Carmelite mystics], and to transmit their profound spiritual and mystical experience." As such, the directors claim to use the term "university" not in the sense of an academic institution but according to the original etymology of the term as a "universal" place of encounter and free thinking, "Because we believe that Mysticism is a 'knowledge' with a particular status which, nonetheless, opens itself to a perspective of interdisciplinary dialogue" that includes "other interlocutors and cultures" so that "Spanish mysticism becomes a capital of humanity."[187] As stated in its mission, the CITeS centers on its Discalced Carmelite heritage and aims at a general, religiously committed public, taking on the goal of promoting the academic study of mysticism and the scholarly work of comparisons across religions. The institution convokes international conferences on comparative religious topics, paying particular attention to the work of the Spanish mystics and other religious and mystical traditions. In 2019, for instance, it celebrated the First World Congress of Jewish and Christian Mysticism, attended by well-known scholars – both religious and lay – from across the world. The goal of the conference was to establish a dialogue between the Jewish Kabbalah tradition and Carmelite mysticism and to understand the theoretical roots and practices that converse between the two traditions. The presentations of the congress were collected in the anthology *Kabbala Judía y Mística Carmelitana: Encuentros en Sefarad*, published by the Center.[188] Likewise, the CITeS hosted, in 2017, "The First World Encounter of Teresian Mysticism and Interreligious Dialogue," which examined the connections between the Carmelite Mysticism and Theravāda Buddhism. Scholars and practitioners of Buddhism, particularly from Europe and Asia, attended the event; and a second "World Encounter" in 2022 has now been announced. The call for conference papers acknowledges the role of interreligious dialogue: "In times of divisions amongst cultures, interreligious dialogue has become an urgent need."[189] These academic events feature innovative meth-

---

Ávila is situated north of Madrid and is where Saint Teresa of Jesus started the reformation of the Discalced Carmelite Order.

187 "Nuestro Ideario," *CITeS Universidada de la Mística*, 2021, https://www.mistica.es/universidad-mistica/ideario-universidad.

188 *Kabbala Judía y Mística Carmelitana: Encuentros en Sefarad* (Burgos, Spain: Editorial Fonte-Monte Carmelo, 2020.)

189 Likewise, the CITeS invites submissions for a prize on comparative religious studies involving the Carmelite mystics and mystical works from other religious traditions.

odologies and practices from the disciplines of comparative literature and comparative theology.

One of the modern scholars whose work in Spanish mystical literature has been published in the acts of the congresses celebrated at the CITeS is the Argentinian scholar Fabio Samuel Esquenazi. Esquenazi's comparative research focuses on Jewish and Spanish mystical literature. His methodology in many ways evokes Luce López-Baralt's and José Ángel Valente's invitation to explore not just historical convergences but the particularities of mystical language. In his article "Las parabolas del *Zohar* y sus resonancias en el *Cántico spiritual*" ("The Parables of the *Zohar* and their resonances in the *Spiritual Canticle*"), Esquenazi compares fragments from the *Sefer ha-Zohar* with two of the main poetical compositions by Saint John of the Cross. The *Sefer ha-Zohar* is a central text of Jewish Kabbalistic mystical literature, composed in Castile during the last three decades of the thirteenth century. This text, Esquenazi argues, shows a "strong association" with Catholic mystical writing, specifically considering the topics of the "clarification of the soul" and the "amorous consummation."[190] Esquenazi skillfully traces the symbol of sight and the different metaphors which define the process of seeing in the *Zohar* and in Saint John of the Cross's poems the *Living Flame of God* and the *Spiritual Canticle*. Keeping the focus on poetic imagery, Esquenazi's question throughout the comparison is not whether Saint John of the Cross read directly the *Sefer ha-Zohar* but how the metaphorical language of the former Jewish text resonates with his poetry. Thus Esquenazi's comparative method is based upon the detailed examination of imagery, which he does not only from the poetic perspective but also by inquiring about the theological Jewish and Christian notions at which the poetic imagery points. He compares the verses and the prose but also delves into discursive strategies, examining the ways in which the authors of *Sefer ha-Zohar* and Saint John of the Cross use very resonant poetic resources to signal equally resonant but distinct theological notions, such as the relationship between the soul and God in both the Kabalistic and the Christian contexts.

A different comparative approach is found in the work of the Cuban-American scholar Gloria Maité Hernández (the present author). In her recent book *Savoring God: Comparative Theopoetics* (2021), Hernández compares the poem *Spiritual Canticle* and its theological commentaries, also composed by Saint John of the Cross, and the Sanskrit poem *Rāsa Līlā* (*The Dance of Divine Love*), originally an oral text put into writing around the thirteenth century,

---

190   Fabio Samuel Esquenazi "Las parabolas del Zohar y sus resonancias en el Cántico espiritual," 423.

alongside two of its main Sanskrit commentaries. The book's methodology, which Hernández describes as a "comparative theopoetics," incorporates aspects from the disciplines of Comparative Literature and Comparative Theology. Seeking to build a self-reflective work of comparison, Hernández states from the beginning of the text that she does not claim historical or philological proximities. Her comparative approach starts from literary, and sometimes philological, analysis of the two poems to then move into the theological inquiry as she attends to the way in which poetry and theology interact with each other. This text-centered methodology, however, does not preclude the author from posing the kind of critical comparative questions that concern modern comparativists in the fields of literature and theology. For Hernández, the comparative theopoetics that her book promotes opens an interdisciplinary and interreligious path going beyond the "post-colonial" backlash that makes scholars refrain for comparisons. With this, she responds not just to post-orientalists' concerns that the act of comparison can become a colonial enterprise but also to the post-colonial fear of engaging with comparisons and being called a "colonialist" scholar. Accordingly, Hernández insists that it is critical for comparativists to acknowledge her or his own biases and assumptions in order to produce a coherent work of scholarship; a comparison that recognizes how we affect and are affected by the act of comparing is an ethical move towards the "post" of the "post-colonial."

To the scholarly field of Spanish mystical literature, modern works such as those by Esquenazi and Hernández contribute new views regarding the orientalist biases of twentieth-century scholars analyzed in this volume. In Esquenazi's work, we do not find an explicit "anxiety of influences," and he does not draw philological-genetic conclusions from the poetic relationship that he sets out to prove. The relation between Spanish mystical literature and orientalism prevails as an assumed question with which the author does not aim to deal. Instead, he attends to the peculiarities of the language that these mystics use. Engaging more explicitly with questions of comparative methodology, Hernández's work brings into the field of Spanish mystical literature critical issues discussed in other disciplines such as comparative theology and comparative literature. In posing such questions – as is also done in this article – Hernández explores how engaging in a truly interdisciplinary dialogue brings renewal to the field of study. It is interesting to notice, in addition, that like Luce López-Baralt, these two authors write from the Americas – not Europe – about Spanish mystical literature. This brings to their work a singular geopolitical and post-colonial connotation that contrasts with the twentieth-century scholarly tendencies discussed here.

One of the challenges of writing the present volume has been to seriously examine the scholarship that preceded us, asking questions that may also affect how we think, write, and teach. While some academics defend – with valid reasons – the need for neutrality between the scholar and the object of study, in analyzing the writings of these scholars it has been difficult to make a clear distinction between the two. While I did not deal with the personalities of the authors whose works I have read and re-read, it was apparent that their orientalist biases, and consequently their work on Spanish mystical literature, had a strong connection with who they were and are as persons, where they lived and worked, and what their personal experiences were throughout a time period that involved two world wars, the devastating Spanish Civil War, and the construction of Spanish democracy. In that sense, this study also questions how useful it is to try to separate who we are from what and how we write and teach.

The most obvious conclusion of this work is the confirmed recognition that the geopolitical biases of twentieth-century scholars affected how they examined Spanish mystical literature. Since their scholarship is foundational for the discipline, how and what they wrote still impacts how and what we think about this subject, so fascinating to many of us. The present volume is, hence, a call to become cognizant of such geopolitical biases so that we may deactivate some of the prejudices that still dominate – and in many ways stagnate – the field of Spanish mystical literature. Yet behind this obvious conclusion, there are other implications, such as attending to the need to continue engaging with other fields of study, de-centralizing, and demystifying the study of mystical literature. When, one hundred years from now, other scholars look back at our work, may they find that we too learned from the past.

Works Cited

Alonso, Dámaso. *La poesía de San Juan de la Cruz (Desde esta ladera)*. Madrid: Editorial Aguilar, 1942.

Anidjar, Gil. "Jewish Mysticism Alterable and Unalterable: On *Orient*ing [sic] Kabbalah Studies and the 'Zohar of Christian Spain.'" *Jewish Social Studies* 3, no. 1 (1996): 89–157.

Asín Palacios, Miguel. *El Islam cristianizado: Estudio del "sufismo" a través de las obras de Abenárabi de Murcia*. Madrid: Editorial Plutarco, 1931.

Asín Palacios, Miguel. "Un precursor hispano musulmán de San Juan de la Cruz." *Al-Andalus*, no. 1 (1933): 7–79.

Cilveti, Ángel L. *Introducción a la mística española*. Madrid: Ediciones Cátedra, 1974.

de Certeau, Michel. *The Mystic Fable: The Sixteenth and Seventeenth Centuries*. Chicago: University of Chicago Press, 1992.

de Certeau, Michel, and Marsanne Brammer. "Mysticism." *Diacritics* 22, no. 2 (Summer, 1992). 13.

de Covarrubias Horozco, Sebastián. *Tesoro de la lengua castellana o española*. Madrid, 1611. https://archive.org/stream/A253315/A253315_djvu.txt.

de la Cruz, Juan. *Cántico espiritual y Comentarios: Obra Completa*. Edited by Luce López Baralt and Eulogio Pacho. Madrid: Alianza Editorial, 2003.

de Nebrija, Antonio. "The Prologue to Grammar of the Castilian Language" (1492). In "On Language and Empire: The Prologue to Grammar of the Castilian Language" (1492). Introduction and translation by Magalí Armillas-Tiseyra. PMLA (*Publication of the Modern Language Association of America*) 131, no. 1 (2016): 197–208.

Domínguez, César. "The South European Orient: A Comparative Reflection on Space in Literary History." *Modern Language Quarterly* 67, no. 4 (2006): 419–449.

Escudero Rodríguez, Javier, ed. *El epistolario (1968–1972): Cartas de Américo Castro y Juan Goytisolo*. Valencia, Spain: Editorial Pre-Textos, 1997.

Esquenazi, Fabio Samuel. "Las parabolas del Zohar y sus resonancias en el Cántico espiritual." In *Actas del III Congreso Mundial Sanjuanista*. Ávila, Spain: Editorial Fonte-Monte Carmelo. Universidad de la Mística, 2019.

Fuchs, Barbara. "Sketches of Spain: Early Modern England's 'Orientalizing' of Iberia." In *Material and Symbolic Circulation between Spain and England, 1554–1604*, edited by Anne Cruz. Aldershot, UK: Ashgate Publishing, 2008.

Green, Otis H. "Notes on the Historical Problem of Castilian Mysticism." *Hispanic Review* 6 (1938): 93–103.

Hatzfeld, Helmut. *Estudios literarios sobre mística española*. Madrid: Editorial Gredos, 1955.

Hernández, Gloria Maité. *Savoring God: Comparative Theopoetics*. New York: Oxford University Press, 2021.

Howarth, David. *The Invention of Spain*. Manchester, UK: Manchester University Press, 2007.

James, William. *The Varieties of Religious Experience: A Study in Human Nature*. New York: Modern Library, 1902.

Katz, Steven T. "Language, Epistemology, and Mysticism." In *Mysticism and Philosophical Analysis*, edited by Steven T. Katz. New York: Oxford University Press, 1978.

Katz, Steven T., ed. *Mysticism and Philosophical Analysis*. New York: Oxford University Press, 1978.

Keller, Carl A. "Mystical Literature." In *Mysticism and Philosophical Analysis*, edited by Steven T. Katz, 94–96. New York: Oxford University Press, 1978.

Kessler, Michael, and Christian Sheppard, eds. Preface to *Mystics: Presence and Aporia*. Chicago: The University of Chicago Press, 2003.

López-Baralt, Luce. *A la zaga de tu huella: La enseñanza de las lenguas semíticas en Salamanca en tiempos de san Juan de la Cruz*. Madrid: Editorial Trotta, 2006.

López-Baralt, Luce. *Asedios a lo indecible: San Juan de la Cruz canta al éxtasis transformante*. Madrid: Editorial Trotta, 1998.

López-Baralt, Luce. *San Juan de la Cruz y el Islam*. México, D. F.: Colegio de México, Centro de Estudios Lingüísticos y Literarios, 1985.

Machado, Antonio. *Nuevas canciones*. Buenos Aires: Alianza Editorial, 2006.

Mackenzie, Ann L., ed. *Spain and its Literature: Essays in Memory of E. Allison Peers*. London: Liverpool University Press, 1997.

Mancho Duque, María Jesús. *El símbolo de la noche en San Juan de la Cruz: Estudio léxico-semántico*. Salamanca: Ediciones Universidad de Salamanca, 1982.

Masuzawa, Tomoko. *The Invention of World Religions: Or, How European Universalism Was Preserved in the Language of Pluralism*. Chicago: The University of Chicago Press, 2005.

McGinn, Bernard. *The Foundations of Mysticism: Origins to the Fifth Century*. Vol. 1. The Presence of God. New York: Crossroad Publishing Company, 1999.

Menéndez Pelayo, Marcelino. "La poesía mística en España." In *La mística española*, edited by Pedro Sáinz Rodríguez. Madrid: Editorial Afrodisio-Aguado, 1956.

Menocal, María Rosa. Review of *Don Miguel Asín Palacios: Mística cristiana y mística musulmana*, by José Valdivia Valor. *Hispanic Review* 64, no. 2 (1996): 259–263.

Menocal, María Rosa. Review of *San Juan de la Cruz y el Islam* and *Huellas del Islam en la literatura española: De Juan Ruiz a Juan Goytisolo*, by Luce López Baralt. *Hispanic Review* 55, no. 3 (1987): 377–380.

Pacho, Eulogio. "Simientes neerlandesas de la mística española." In *Fuentes neerlandesas de la mística española*, edited by Miguel N. Ubarri and Lieve Behiels. Madrid: Editorial Trotta, 2005.

Peers, Edgar Allison. "Contemporary Spain: Legend and Reality." *Books Abroad* 8, no. 1 (1934): 3–4.

Peers, Edgar Allison. "Notes on the Historical Problem of Castilian Mysticism." *Hispanic Review* 10, no. 1 (1942) 18–33.

Peers, Edgar Allison. *Spanish Mysticism: A Preliminary Survey*. London: Methuen Publishing, Ltd., 1924.

Peers, Edgar Allison. *Studies of the Spanish Mystics*. New York: The Macmillan Company, 1927.

Peers, Edgar Allison. "The Alleged Debts of San Juan de la Cruz to Boscán and Garcilaso de la Vega." *Hispanic Review* 21, no. 1 (1953): 1–19.

Peers, Edgar Allison. "The Alleged Debts of San Juan de la Cruz to Boscán and Garcilaso de la Vega (Concluded)." *Hispanic Review* 21, no. 2 (1953): 93–106.

Said, Edward. *Orientalism*. New York: Vintage Books, 1994.
Sáinz Rodríguez, Pedro, ed. *La mística española*, Madrid: Editorial Afrodisio-Aguado, 1956.
Streng, Frederick. "Language and Mystical Awareness." In *Mysticism and Philosophical Analysis*, edited by Steven T. Katz, 141–152. New York: Oxford University Press, 1978.
Thompson, Colin P. *The Poet and the Mystic: A Study of the Cántico Espiritual of San Juan de la Cruz*. Oxford: Oxford University Press, 1977.
Underhill, Evelyn. *Mysticism: The Development of Humankind's Spiritual Consciousness*. New York: Noonday Press, 1955.
Underhill, Evelyn. Review of *Mysticism East and West: A Comparative Analysis of the Nature of Mysticism*, by Rudolf Otto. *Philosophy* 7, no. 27 (1932) 485–486.
Valente, José Ángel. "Formas de lectura y dinámica de la tradición." In *Hermenéutica y mística: San Juan de la Cruz*, edited by José Ángel Valente and José Lara Garrido, 15–22. Madrid: Editorial Tecnos, 1995.
Valente, José Ángel. "Sobre el lenguaje de los místicos: convergencia y transmission." In *Variaciones del pájaro y la red: Obras Completas II*. Barcelona: Galaxia Gutenberg. Círculo de Lectores, 2008.
Valente, José Ángel. "La hermenéutica y la cortedad del decir." In *Las palabras de la tribu: Obras Completas II*. Barcelona: Galaxia Gutenberg. Círculo de Lectores, 2008.
Valente, José Ángel. "*Verbum absconditum*." In *Variaciones sobre el pájaro y la red: Obras Completas II*. Barcelona: Galaxia Gutenberg. Círculo de Lectores, 2008.
Valente, José Ángel. "El ojo del agua." In *La Piedra y el centro: Obras Completas II*. Barcelona: Galaxia Gutenberg. Círculo de Lectores, 2008.
Valente, José Ángel. and José Lara Garrido, eds. *Hermenéutica y mística: San Juan de la Cruz*. Madrid: Editorial Tecnos, 1995.
Varisco, Daniel M. *Reading Orientalism: Said and the Unsaid*. Seattle: University of Washington Press, 2007.

General Bibliography

Altamira, Rafael. *Psicología del pueblo español*. Madrid: Librería de Fernando Fé, 1902.
Asín Palacios, Miguel. *Las Huellas del Islam*. Madrid: Editorial Espasa-Calpe, 1941.
Asín Palacios, Miguel. *Sadilíes y alumbrados*. Madrid: Ediciones Hiperión, 1990.
Baruzi, Jean. *Saint Jean de la Croix et le problème de l'expérience mystique*. Paris: Librairie Félix Alcan, 1924.
Bataillon, Marcel. *Erasme et l'Espagne: Recherches sur l'histoire spirituelle du XVIe siècle*. Paris: Librairie E. Droz, 1937.

Bell, Aubrey F. G. "Notes on the Spanish Renaissance." *Revue Hispanique* 80, no. 178 (1930): 526.

Bloom, Harold. *The Anxiety of Influence: A Theory of Poetry*. New York: Oxford University Press, 1973.

Corriente, Federico. *Poesía Dialectal Árabe y Romance en Alandalús*. Madrid: Editorial Gredos, 1997.

de Jesús, Crisógono. *Vida de San Juan de la Cruz*. San Sebastián, Spain: Gráficas Fides, 1941.

de Jesús, Crisógono. *The Life of St. John of the Cross*. Translated by Kathleen Pond. New York: Harper and Brothers, 1958.

de Nebrija, Antonio. *Gramática de la Lengua Castellana*. Madrid: Joachin de Ibarra, 1492.

Gálvez, Manuel. *El solar de la raza*. Madrid: Saturnino Calleja, 1920.

Ganivet, Ángel. *Idearium Español*. Madrid: Librería General de Victoriano Suarez, 1897.

García Gómez, Emilio. *Las jarchas romances de la serie árabe en su marco*. Barcelona: Editorial Seix Barral, 1975.

Groult, Pierre. *Les mystiques des Pays-Bas e la litérature espagnole du seizième siècle*. Louvain: Librairie Universitaire, 1927.

Guillén, Jorge. *Lenguaje y poesía: Algunos casos españoles*. Madrid: Revista de Occidente, 1962.

Inge, William Ralph. *Christian Mysticism: Considered in Eight Lectures Delivered Before the University of Oxford*. London: Methuen & Co., 1899.

Kabbala Judía y Mística Carmelitana: Encuentros en Sefarad. Javier Sancho Fermín, Director. Ávila, Spain: Grupo Editorial Fonte-Monte Carmelo. Universidad de la Mística, 2020.

Llull, Raymond. *The Book of the Lover and the Beloved*. Translated by Edgar Allison Peers. New York: The Macmillan Company, 1923.

López Baralt, Luce, and Gloria Maité Hernández, eds. *Miguel Asín Palacios: Estudiante de lengua sánscrita y profesor de la filosofía religiosa de la India*. Madrid: Mandala Ediciones, 2015.

Martín Velasco, Juan. *El fenómeno místico: Estudio comparado*. Madrid: Editorial Trotta, 1999.

Massignon, Louis. "Textes musulmans pouvant concerner la nuit de l'espirit." *Études Carmélitaines mystiques et missionnaires*, October 1938.

Menéndez Pelayo, Marcelino. *Historia de las ideas estéticas en España*. 8 vols. Madrid: Imprenta de A. Pérez Dubrull, 1883–1891.

Menéndez Pelayo, Marcelino. *Historia de los heterodoxos españoles*. Madrid: Librería Católica de San José, 1880.

Otto, Rudolf. *Mysticism East and West: A Comparative Analysis of the Nature of Mysticism*. London: The Macmillan Company, 1932.

Pfandl, Ludwig. *Historia de la literatura nacional española en la edad de oro*. Edited by Lorenzo Cortina. Barcelona: Sucesores de Juan Gili, 1933.

Pfleiderer, Otto. *Religion and Historic Faiths*. Translated by Daniel A. Huebsch. New York: B. W. Huebsch, 1907.

Sáinz y Rodríguez, Pedro. "El problema histórico del misticismo español." *Revista de Occidente* 5, no. 45 (1927).

Scholem, Gershom. *Major Trends in Jewish Mysticism*. Jerusalem: Schocken Publishing House, 1941.

Stern, Samuel Miklos. "Les vers finaux en espagnol dans les muwassahs hispanohebraïques." *Al-Andalus* 13 (1948), 299–346.

Teresa of Jesus. *The Way of Perfection*. In *The Complete Works of Saint Teresa of Jesus*. 2 vols. Translated by Edgar Allison Peers. New York: Sheed and Ward, 1946.

Thompson Colin P. *The Poet and the Mystic*. Oxford: Oxford University Press, 1977.

Valbuena, José Ángel. *Antología de poesía sacra española*. Barcelona: Editorial Apolo, 1940.

Zaehner, Robert Charles. *Mysticism Sacred and Profane: An Inquiry into Some Varieties of Praeternatural Experience*. Oxford: Clarendon Press, 1957.

Printed in the United States
by Baker & Taylor Publisher Services